100 Ideas for
Secondary Teachers

Outstanding History Lessons

Emily Thomas

B L O O M S B U R Y
LONDON · OXFORD · NEW YORK · NEW DELHI · SYDNEY

BLOOMSBURY EDUCATION
Bloomsbury Publishing Plc
50 Bedford Square, London, WC1B 3DP, UK
1385 Broadway, New York, NY 10018, USA
29 Earlsfort Terrace, Dublin 2, Ireland

BLOOMSBURY, BLOOMSBURY EDUCATION and the Diana logo
are trademarks of Bloomsbury Publishing Plc

First published in Great Britain 2017

Copyright © Emily Thomas, 2017

All rights reserved. No part of this publication may be reproduced or
transmitted in any form or by any means, electronic or mechanical,
including photocopying, recording, or any information storage or
retrieval system, without prior permission in writing from the publishers.

A catalogue record for this book is available from the British Library.

Library of Congress Cataloguing-in-Publication data has been
applied for.

ISBN:
PB 9781472940957
ePub 9781472940933
ePDF 9781472940964

4 6 8 10 9 7 5

Typeset by Newgen Knowledge Works (P) Ltd., Chennai, India
Printed and bound by CPI Group (UK) Ltd, Croydon, CR0 4YY

This book is produced using paper that is made from wood grown in
managed, sustainable forests. It is natural, renewable and recyclable. The
logging and manufacturing processes conform to the environmental
regulations of the country of origin.

To find out more about our authors and books visit
www.bloomsbury.com. Here you will find extracts, author interviews,
details of forthcoming events and the option to sign up for
our newsletters.

Contents

Acknowledgements

Sincere thanks to those whose ideas I have used or adapted, especially Russel Tarr, Carol Stobbs, Richard Kennett, Scott Allsop, John Mitchell, Greg Thornton, Katie Hunter, Andy Harmsworth, Joel Thorpe, Lucie Barber and Katie Thoburn. Thank you to the young people who agreed to be interviewed, especially Maisie, Zoe, Mustafa, Finn, Casey, Luke and Sabrina. Many of the best ideas come from colleagues past and present, particularly Paige Richardson, and I am grateful to my current team: Mary Feerick; Bea Honap-Baker; Katie Thoburn and John Chescoe, for always being willing to share and discuss teaching ideas. A number of academics were kind enough to offer their views on what makes for outstanding history teaching, including Darius Jackson, Peter Vass and Ian Grosvenor. Thank you to my partner, Pete, for the time and support; to my mum, Maria, for the many hours of childcare; and my dad, Gary, for the tips and edits. I'm also very grateful to Rhiannon Findlay at Bloomsbury for her patience and thoughtful advice.

Introduction

As history teachers, we naturally want to offer our students outstanding lessons – 'outstanding' not only in the sense that they fulfil the official criteria for 'outstanding', but also in the sense that they fire curiosity, 'make pennies drop' and challenge assumptions. At its best, history education is not only intellectually transformative, it is exciting and enjoyable.

I hope that this book will help teachers offer history lessons that speak to both sides of 'outstanding' – to be inspiring at the same time as meeting formal criteria. In it, I hope to offer guidance on the teaching of historical processes and macro-historical thinking, as well as the teaching of detailed subject knowledge, and to help make this teaching engaging and inclusive.

While this book contains ideas for activities, it's important to stress that outstanding lessons are not characterised by what students do in the course of a lesson but rather by what they learn and understand. I suggest that you plan each lesson by first determining the knowledge, skills and understanding that you want students to gain from it. Only then can you work out the best way to achieve those outcomes. This may sound obvious, but it can be tempting to try to plan an outstanding lesson by packing it full of 'whizzy' activities. A lesson in which students recreate Agincourt with Jelly Babies and Super Soakers may look impressive (and be very popular with students) but is not necessarily outstanding – in any sense.

It is also worth stressing that a lesson is an interaction, not a performance: outstanding lessons are not over-planned, leaving time for plenty of teacher-student dialogue in recognition of the fact that you, the teacher – with your knowledge, skills and enthusiasm – are the most valuable resource in the room.

Acknowledging the artificiality of snapshot observation, Ofsted no longer grades individual lessons during inspections. While some schools continue to do so through internal observation, Ofsted's move is a useful reminder that what matters is what students learn. How you help them learn it is up to you.

I think that students learn best when they are challenged but not threatened, when learning activities are varied and memorable and when everyone in the room is included. It is with this in mind that I have selected ideas for this book. There may be some you have seen elsewhere and others that aren't quite for you, but I hope that there is plenty here that you can put to use.

How to use this book

This book includes quick, easy and practical ideas for you to dip in and out of, to support you in teaching secondary history.

Each idea includes:

- A catchy title, easy to refer to and share with your colleagues.
- An interesting quote linked to the idea.
- A summary of the idea in bold, making it easy to flick through the book and identify an idea you want to use at a glance.
- A step-by-step guide to implementing the idea.

Each idea also includes one or more of the following:

Teaching tip	Taking it further	Bonus idea ★
Some extra advice on how or how not to run the activity or put the strategy into practice.	Ideas and advice for how to extend the idea or develop it further.	There are 55 bonus ideas in this book that are extra exciting and extra original.

Online resources also accompany this book. When online resources are referenced in the book, follow the link, www.bloomsbury.com/100-ideas-secondary-history, to find extra resources, catalogued under the relevant idea number.

Share how you use these ideas in the classroom and find out what other teachers have done using #100ideas.

Big, bold historical thinking: second-order concepts in the classroom

Part 1

Recipes for change

'Place 100,000 migrant workers into a small city. Drop in a handful of dissidents and sprinkle with a pinch of revolutionary literature. Bring to the boil, stirring continuously.'

This activity from Katie Thoburn involves analysing the run up to an historical event. It works particularly well with younger students who enjoy the imaginative element.

Teaching tip

Younger students enjoy illustrating their recipes for homework. A fun twist involves students presenting their recipes in the style of TV chefs.

Show students a recipe for sponge cake, and talk about how the end product is a result of the way that the ingredients interact.

Apply this to the event you are studying by asking them to list its historical 'ingredients' (i.e. the factors that caused it).

Students can then think about the way that those ingredients combined to bring about the event in question, and produce a sequence of instructions in the style of a recipe. The command words common to recipes, such as sprinkle, stir, spread, and remove make it easy for students to come up with analogies, and will help them remember the historical factors later on.

In this example the recipe produces the Great Fire of London:

1. Take a network of narrow streets and pack as tightly as possible with timber buildings.
2. Sprinkle liberally with flammable ingredients.
3. Leave mixture to dry out thoroughly (one very hot summer should do it).
4. Throw in a strong easterly wind.
5. Drop in a spark.
6. Stand back!

Taking it further

Ask students to consider whether all ingredients and stages are equally important, prompting a more complex discussion about the nature of causation.

Change over time: the historical road map

'Roadblocks; diversions; bridges; shortcuts ... the possibilities for historical metaphors are endless.'

Ask students to draw giant 'road maps' — visual representations of the process of historical change — for the metaphorical journeys of groups or individuals in the past.

This activity, inspired by a tweet from @aheadofhistory, allows students to examine the complex nature of change; how it speeds up and slows down, and how it can be hampered or facilitated by external factors. It can also be used to examine the quest of an individual — such as Henry VIII's pursuit of his first divorce — or used to illustrate a much broader change, such as the development of public health.

Here are some ideas to get your students started:

- Problems or obstacles along the route can be represented by pot holes, steep hills, road blocks or dead ends.
- Represent factors which helped to speed up or enable change with shortcuts and bypasses.
- Changes in the approach to the journey itself can be represented by diversions or lane changes (my students had Thomas Cromwell off-roading completely during the break from Rome).
- Changes to those leading the journey or advising on it can be represented by changing who is driving or map-reading.
- The different approaches of different groups involved in the journey can be represented by their being more than one route on the map.

Teaching tip

This idea works particularly well when you are looking at a prolonged struggle by a group in history to achieve something specific. Think about what the Civil Rights Movement or the campaign for female suffrage might look like when presented as a road map.

Bonus idea ★

Photograph students' maps and project them onto the whiteboard (or use a visualiser if you have one), to allow students to talk their classmates through their representations of the process examined.

Causal spider webs

'The study of history is a study of causes.' (E.H. Carr)

When teaching them to construct meaningful historical explanations, we want students to analyse, rather than merely list, the causes of historical events and developments. The process of creating causal webs gets students thinking about how causes relate to each other.

Teaching tip

Letting students fill in the 'cause' boxes themselves will help consolidate their knowledge of the narrative content.

After putting the central event (the one they are trying to explain) in the middle of the page, students surround it with boxes containing all the causes of the event.

All of these cause boxes will be linked to the central event, but many will also be linked to each other. As students consider these links, they should draw lines between the various causes, and something resembling a messy web will take shape. They must then write along these lines to explain their links. This example shows a causal web for the 1905 Russian Revolution, with political and economic causes and triggers shaded differently. For clarity, only one of the linking lines is annotated.

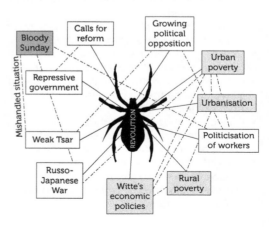

You could also ask students to look at the causes and see if they can identify types or categories. These might include:

- short or long term causes
- triggers or underlying causes
- individual or group agency
- deliberate or non-deliberate action.

Ask them to shade or label the boxes to show the different types of causes.

Bonus idea

Consider making causal webs directly on the table tops, using dry-wipe markers for the lines and sticky notes for the causes. This makes it easier for students to move around and group causes, and will help them to review and change connections.

Historical hexagons

'Hexagon configuration tasks enable the categorising and linking processes that are part of good historical analysis.'

So-called 'hexagonal learning' is a way of physically organising pieces of information to promote deeper, more analytical thinking. The idea comes from Damian Clark (invisiblelearning. blogspot.co.uk).

Teaching tip

If the thought of 'faffing around' with scissors and glue puts you off, try Russel Tarr's online hexagon generator at www.classtools.net/ hexagon, and get students dragging and dropping virtual hexagons.

Give students a sheet with multiple hexagons on it (around 14 works well). Each hexagon should contain a piece of information, such as a topic word or sentence. Ask the students to cut these hexagons out. You may choose to get the students involved in coming up with the words or sentences, or provide them with 'pre-filled' hexagons.

They must now fit them back together, but the hexagons can only touch one another where students can justify a link or connection. You will end up with variously-shaped groups of hexagons. Some hexagons will be connected to others on all sides, some might join as a line, and others might stand out completely on their own.

Example 1 looks at the various features characterising Weimar culture and society between 1924 and 1929. How might students examining the interconnectivity of these features configure the hexagons?

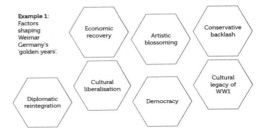

Example 1: Factors shaping Weimar Germany's 'golden years'.

Economic recovery

Artistic blossoming

Conservative backlash

Cultural liberalisation

Democracy

Cultural legacy of WW1

Diplomatic reintegration

Example 2 shows how a series of hexagons on the factors leading up to the Peasants' Revolt might look once configured by students.

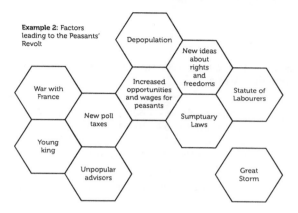

Example 2: Factors leading to the Peasants' Revolt

Depopulation

New ideas about rights and freedoms

War with France

Increased opportunities and wages for peasants

Statute of Labourers

New poll taxes

Sumptuary Laws

Young king

Unpopular advisors

Great Storm

Students should annotate their configured hexagons to explain their links, paying particular attention to the points where three meet; it is here that they will often draw out important and overarching themes.

Hexagon-based tasks lend themselves well to differentiation. There is no correct arrangement – in fact, it is very rare for two students to come up with the same arrangement of hexagons.

For an easy to use template, go to http://pamhook.com/solo-apps/hexagon-generator/. You can populate and then print a sheet of hexagons in a couple of minutes.

> **Bonus idea** ★
>
> John Mitchell recommends images in place of words. Students have to interpret the pictures first, adding an extra dimension.

Causal equations

'It all adds up.'

Provide students with 'factor cards' and 'function cards', and get them producing historical sums.

Taking it further

Causal equations are useful in isolating 'linchpin' causes, and are great when exploring counterfactual history (see Idea 14: The counterfactual fan).

Function cards (+, − and =) help students fit historical factors together to explore, explain and predict scenarios. The idea is inspired by the 'logic sums' task tweeted by @rusheymeadhist.

Give students plenty of each of these function cards:

Factor cards are specific to the topic. This example set could be used to examine the impact of any historical economic shock. What kinds of 'equations' could be made from the example cards exploring the impact of World War II on the US economy?

The following example, using the same cards, is a simplified causal equation on the impact of the Black Death:

I have used similar factor cards in a GCSE activity looking at the Wall Street Crash. Students become presidential advisers, arranging the cards to explain the reasons for the boom, the impact of the crash and finally to explore the potential impact of various courses of governmental action.

This task works particularly well with economic history because of the measurable nature of the factors involved, but causal equations can be used to explore the interaction of factors involved in a whole range of historical processes. How about using different factor cards to explain the burgeoning or quelling of popular dissent or the expansion or contraction of an empire?

Getting creative with links: paper causation chains and paper-chain people

'A fun but challenging activity (which produces great classroom decorations).'

Make physical representations of historical change out of paper chains, asking students to identify and explain the links.

Teaching tip

When making paperchain people, students often identify figures that influenced numerous lines of thought or paths of action. Provide sticky tape and explain that the chains do not need to be neat or linear.

Causation chains: Get a few packs of DIY lick-and-stick paper chains, or just some sugar paper and glue, and get students creating paper-chain representations of historical causation. Create long strands of these with every other hoop being an explanation of the link between the two it joins together. Or, to borrow the fantastic idea tweeted by Dan Kearney (@history_of_dan), create chaotic-looking but more realistic causation chains by having many paper chains connected to a central hoop symbolising the key event. A central '1965 Voting Rights Act' hoop, for example, would have various chains of causation leading to it (perhaps one to signify presidential action, one to signify peaceful protest, and so forth). Inevitably, these causation chains will also be linked at various points.

Paper-chain people: In this activity from Russel Tarr, students make paper-chain people to illustrate how individuals are able to bring about historical change by building on the work of others. Students fold and cut paper to make strings of people joined by the hands. Having made a paper chain – for example of the most important figures in the history of medicine – students stick or draw the faces of the people involved in chronological order, using the arms to note how they built on or contributed to the work of those before and after them.

Taking it further

Use completed chains as stimulus material for longer written pieces or to give structure to short presentations.

The rollercoaster graph: examining change

'Napoleon's rollercoaster looks terrifying!'

Examine change over time by giving it visual representation in the form of a 'living' graph. Ask your students to draw their graphs as rollercoasters, with carriages containing the people affected by the historical change in question.

Use the living or rollercoaster graph to plot the key events within a topic on a timeline (the X axis) while using the Y axis to make historical judgements about the events. You could, for example, create a graph to examine Henry VIII's foreign policy, with success and failure on the Y axis. During times when Henry's foreign policy was getting the desired results, the line (or rollercoaster track) goes up. When things go wrong, it comes crashing down.

The rollercoaster graph works well when you want to compare the experiences of different people. When studying prosperity and poverty in 1920s America, my students make different rollercoasters for different social groups. It is also useful for examining the role of individuals in a particular development or series of events. Which advisers could be found in the carriage riding alongside Henry VIII at different points on his foreign policy rollercoaster?

Students can annotate their graphs to add historical detail about and explanations for the events and changes shown.

This can be done as a one-off extended activity, or it might be something you build up over a series of lessons, perhaps becoming part of a regular plenary task. The finished result is an excellent starting point for a written piece and a useful revision tool.

Teaching tip

For an example of a rollercoaster graph see www.bloomsbury.com/100-ideas-secondary-history/.

Taking it further

Let the students decide which events to include and, in doing so, encourage them to think about the concept of historical significance (see Idea 8: Discussing and debating historical significance using a radar diagram).

Bonus idea ★

Fancy a change from pen and paper? www.classtools.net has a living graph generator, allowing students to make electronic versions, while @lesleymunroe4 uses pipe cleaners to make 3-D versions.

Discussing and debating historical significance using a radar diagram

'Why is there a longer Wikipedia article about Victoria Beckham than Ada Lovelace?'

Get students to think about what determines historical significance and use a radar diagram to evaluate the significance of the people and events they are studying.

Teaching tip

By switching to different coloured pens for different events or individuals, you can use the same diagram to make direct comparisons.

It is important not only that students understand why some things are deemed more historically significant than others, but also that the answer to the question 'how significant was X?' depends to a large extent on who is answering it and in what context.

Determining historical significance

Ask students to come up with ideas about what makes something historically significant. You may need to start them off with an example. Compare the results of their discussions to the criteria laid out by Partington in *The Idea of An Historical Education* (1980). They are:

- **Importance:** How important was the event deemed to be at the time?
- **Profundity:** How deeply were people's lives affected?
- **Quantity:** How many people were affected?
- **Durability:** For how long were people's lives affected?
- **Relevance:** How interesting or useful is it in terms of the increased understanding of the present?

Stuart Godman (@aheadofhistory) has developed a fantastic diagram to help students visualise this. Students draw a radar chart with five spokes, each of which is an axis to measure the subject matter against one of Partington's five criteria. The resultant diagram looks a bit like a spider's web.

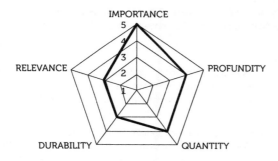

Taking it further

Significance makes good subject matter for challenging extension questions. How far do students agree with Partington's criteria for historical significance? Even if we use fixed criteria like Partington's to determine historical significance, can this process ever be objective?

13

The significance tournament

'You can never bring too many football analogies to the classroom...'

This is a fun and lively way of debating historical significance as a whole class, using a football-style tournament wall chart to provide structure.

Teaching tip

Older students can be encouraged to do this in groups of eight, with each individual arguing for a particular factor.

Taking it further

Ask your students if they agree with the result that the chart produces. If not, what are the flaws in this way of determining significance? (For example, it doesn't allow for the fact that some factors are interlinked.)

This activity comes from Scott Allsop, and a template wall chart can be accessed on his blog: http://www.mrallsophistory.com/revision/.

Break your class into eight small groups and assign each group an historical factor. The group must prepare to argue that their factor is more significant than the other seven, in relation to the bigger historical issue you are examining.

Once the groups have prepared their cases, initiate a whole-class 'tournament' in which the ideas are pitted against each other in a series of mini-debates, each seeing one of the factors knocked out of the tournament, until you are left with only one factor at the end – theoretically the most significant.

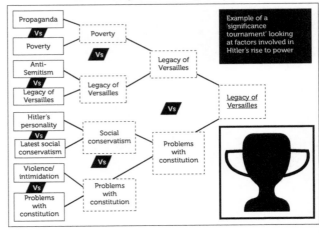

Making time to think: The flipped history classroom model

'"Flipped-learning" sounds like something faddy or complicated. Actually, it's incredibly straightforward, and for a subject like history with so much content to cover, can be really useful.'

Maximise time for historical thinking by using the flipped model to deliver narrative content in advance of the lesson.

Good story-telling is part of the joy of teaching history. But overdoing it can turn students off and excessive teacher talk is one of the most common criticisms levelled by observers at observees. If we limit our verbal exposition, not only are we more likely to keep students' attention when we *do* have reason to speak to them at length, but we also free up time for the exploration of the abstract ideas integral to the study of history.

But students can't do anything meaningful in history lessons without historical knowledge. This is where the flipped learning model helps. You increase the time you have with students to probe and extend their historical understanding by asking them to look over the narrative content as homework, in advance of the lesson. It can be as simple as setting them a bit of reading to do at home, but many teachers now upload their PowerPoints to the internet with recorded explanations to accompany each slide (see Idea 85: Using ICT to achieve a flipped learning classroom).

Having thoroughly checked student knowledge and addressed any misconceptions at the start of the following lesson, you can launch into activities that require students to apply their new knowledge.

Teaching Tip

Use a selection of quick learning checks (see Idea 61: Quick progress checks) as a starter and employ some targeted questioning (see Idea 12: Clever question stems) to ensure that everyone has got what they need from the flipped learning tasks. Do not move on until you are confident that everyone is comfortable with the content.

Thoughtful historical discussion: speaking prompt cards

'These cards are quick to make and have endless uses.'

Create two sets of cards, the first bearing speaking prompts and the second bearing topic words, for use in a variety of thought-provoking activities.

Speaking prompts are words or phrases which encourage students to construct explanations and link various aspects of their knowledge. In all of the activities suggested below, students have to build statements which include both speaking prompts and topic words. Importantly, their statements can also contain as many other words as they like.

Suggested speaking prompts (these cards are available on the companion website, www.bloomsbury.com/100-ideas-secondary-history):

- Because
- Although
- It is possible that
- This meant that
- Including
- Led to
- However
- The combination of ... and ...
- Therefore.

'Whistory' (a bit like whist, but with history ...):
Players get a hand in which they have a mixture of speaking prompts and topic cards. They form a 'trick' by creating a statement including *at least* one card of each type. The objective is to get rid of your hand.

Bonus idea ★

Vary the speaking prompt and topic word cards to differentiate this activity.

In a game with topic words on Germany after World War I, a statement might be as simple as *'Because of* the harsh terms imposed at Versailles, Germany saw an upsurge in *nationalism.'* If the player wanted to get rid of more cards, he or she could form a much longer sentence. Get players to time their opponents (otherwise students will spend an age composing multi-clause sentences to win outright in one go!). Thirty seconds to a minute is usually enough.

Pair or pass: Put the speaking prompt cards face-down in one pile and the topic cards in another. Students take one card from each pile. If they can form a statement they may keep the pair; if not, they must pass it to another player to have a go.

Prompt cards only: Keep your prompt cards not only for reuse in games, but to help you check knowledge and understanding. You might, for example, ask pairs or groups to isolate ten words that sum up a reading they have done for homework, and then give out sets of speaking prompt cards to use in conjunction with their chosen terms.

Teaching Tip

Instead of putting them on cards, select six speaking prompts and display them on the board, numbered one to six. Students throw a die and make a sentence about the topic they are studying, using the speaking prompt correlating to the number they roll.

Clever question stems

'Questioning is about more than finding out how much students know: it's about asking them to think.'

Effective questioning is a crucial feature of outstanding lessons and a versatile teaching tool. Use it to check learning, challenge preconceptions, promote higher-order thinking and encourage students to grapple with the nature of history.

Teaching tip

As an interesting exercise, try ticking names off a list each time you speak to a student over the course of a lesson. Do you allocate your attention fairly? The results can be surprising.

Targeted questioning is also the simplest form of differentiation: by planning your questions you can ensure that you stretch pupils of all levels.

We all use closed questions (asking, for example, when something happened or where) to check that key information has been retained. The trick is to move quickly on to more open questions of the kind that require students to really engage their brains.

The following question 'stems' are suggested starting points

Ask students to consider why events played out as they did. For example:

- Why do you think ... took this course of action?
- How might things have been different if ...?

Probe them on the significance of the subject matter and how it links to prior learning. For example:

- What does ... tell us about ...?
- How does what we have learnt today confirm or contradict what we already know about ...?

Ask them to think about the place of the subject matter within history and its treatment at the hands of historians. For example:

- Why do you think ... is studied in schools today?
- Do you suppose that attitudes towards ... have changed much over time, and if so, how?
- What do you suppose have been the most important sources of evidence for historians studying ...? What impact might this have had on what has been written about it?
- Do you have any unanswered questions about ... and if so, what kinds of sources might help you answer them?
- Which aspects of ... are most open to interpretation?
- Are there any groups who might disagree with this interpretation of ...?

Bonus idea ★

Assign a different thought-provoking question about the previous lesson's learning to each pair or threesome at the start of the lesson. Give them a couple of minutes to discuss it and then seek verbal feedback.

Linking games

'Making links between different aspects of historical knowledge encourages mental agility and helps students draw out themes.'

In these two games, students need to employ flexible thinking in order to makes links between things that may at first appear to be only indirectly connected.

Roll and link

Make a grid of six by six and in each box write key terms or names of individuals involved in the period or topic you are studying (you can prepare this ahead or get the students to do it themselves). Students roll two dice to direct them to random squares on the grid (if I rolled a four and a six, I would count up four and along six).They must then create a sentence or two to explain how these things are linked. On a grid themed around Russia during World War, students might land first on Tannenberg and then on Rasputin, and, after a bit of thought, come up with something like, 'After the Russian army experienced defeats like Tannenberg, Nicholas II made the decision to assume supreme command of the Russian forces. In his absence the Tsarina fell back on Rasputin's advice.'

Link dominoes

Students make domino cards, each featuring any two terms or names, which may only be connected to another domino if they can come up with a linking sentence to justify the connection.

Taking it further

Students should note the best sentences as they go, and to be ready to share them. If there are any pairs of words that they cannot link, they should also note these down and put them to the class during the feedback session to see if anyone else can suggest link.

Bonus idea ★

Create giant link dominos and allocate one per student, asking them to stand in a logical order at the front of the classroom.

The counterfactual fan

'By imagining what could have happened, we see the significance of what did happen.'

Ask students to plot the many different paths history could have taken were one key factor altered, before choosing one of these paths and writing the alternative version of events.

How might things have been different if Hitler had been killed in the July Bomb Plot, or if President John F. Kennedy had cancelled his November 1963 trip to Dallas? To construct plausible answers to such questions, students must draw deeply on their knowledge of a period. This is a challenging activity, particularly suited to sixth-formers, and makes a good extension task.

First, ask students to write the altered event (for example 'Catherine of Aragon bears a healthy male heir') in a box on the far left-hand side of the page, halfway down.

They should draw two to four branches coming out of their main box, and, at the end of each branch, write a plausible consequence of the counterfactual event (for example, 'Catherine's influence at court is strengthened'). Students should then add consequence branches to each of these scenarios (perhaps, 'Henry develops a lasting alliance with Charles V').

What students end up with is a flow diagram which looks like a fan (although they will often end up focusing on one branch and abandoning the others, which is fine). They must then choose one chain of counterfactual events from their diagram and write an alternative history of the period or topic on no more than two sides of paper. This makes a good homework task, and students enjoy reading and arguing about each other's counterfactual histories in the follow up session.

Teaching Tip

There are plenty of free online flowchart generators you can use to make your counterfactual fans. Try www.gliffy.com.

Taking it further

Older students should be encouraged to think about the controversy surrounding counterfactual history: is it just fun speculation or does it serve a purpose? *The Guardian*'s review of Richard J. Evans's book on the subject: *Altered Pasts: Counterfactuals in History* offers a neat summary to help them access the debate: www.theguardian.com/books/2014/apr/17/altered-pasts-counterfactuals-in-history-review.

Making history: the role of evidence and the construction of historical interpretation

Part 2

Teaching with historical sources

'Histories unrooted in evidence are just stories.'

Learning to use historical evidence is at the very heart of a good history education. This page deals with the principles and priorities of teaching with historical sources.

Teaching tip

Dividing historical evidence into primary and secondary sources can prove unhelpful. There is no clear dividing line and students need to bring the same critical skills to bear when analysing sources from any period.

Attempts to harness and simplify the processes of historical research for the classroom have resulted in an artificial sub-discipline within secondary school history: 'source work'. At its worst, source work is a tedious process in which students use preselected sources to get at predetermined 'correct' answers, mindful only that if a source turns out to be 'biased' it is a red-herring and must be written off.

It's our job to make source analysis less mechanistic and more realistic (and therefore more exciting) and to convey to our students the central role of evidence in history, bringing it to the heart of our teaching.

Bring discussion of evidence into narrative exposition: Tear down the artificial boundary between source work and narrative history. What's wrong with stopping mid description of the spread of venereal disease in World War I to ask how on earth historians find out about this sort of stuff? The answer is never simple and often illuminating, provoking further questions about the nature of the history being studied. For pointers on challenging discussions on the making of history see Idea 33: On Tuesday 13 January, 1671, a flea farted. Is this history? and Idea 35: The history vs. story Venn diagram.

Look for and tackle student misconceptions:
The idea that there is a single, correct version of the past waiting to be uncovered is a real stumbling block for young people and is the root of other common misunderstandings, such as the idea that sources are intrinsically good or bad. Emphasise and re-emphasise that sources do not have fixed qualities in terms of reliability or usefulness – the nature of the evidence they offer depends on the question being asked. Tasks helping to underscore this point include Idea 16: Call the COP – a source analysis and evaluation rubric and Idea 22: Skip diving for 'rubbish' sources.

Get students constructing and testing their own theories about the past: It is possible to get secondary-aged students forming and honing historical questions, identifying the evidence they need to answer them, locating this evidence and using it to answer their own questions. This process is part and parcel of A level coursework, but can be promoted further down the school too. Local research projects are an ideal way to get students conducting authentic historical research. See Idea 83: Embracing diverse histories and Idea 97: Local history walks. Lessons that ask students to construct and defend evidence-based cases – including Idea 27: Police investigations and Idea 32: Historical figures on trial – while less reflective of 'real life' historical research, are useful in building related skills.

Use rubrics and tables to guide rather than lead your students: There's no denying that rubrics and formulae are useful in that they help students remember the steps involved in analysing and evaluating sources. What's important is that the rubrics are seen by students as tools only – starting points, rather than ends in themselves.

Bonus idea ★

It can be helpful to use non-historical examples when introducing students to ideas about evidence. I ask younger groups to think about how a teacher might investigate a food fight in the school canteen, using this as a springboard into a discussion about the usefulness and reliability of sources.

Call the COP – a source analysis and evaluation rubric

'Sources aren't evidence until they're used to answer historical questions. The nature and strength of the evidence they provide depends on the question.'

The COP board takes account of the fact that working with an historical source involves two important stages: first, students must identify the intrinsic properties of a source and then, more importantly, consider the implications of these properties for the specific historical investigation being undertaken.

Teaching tip

Ask students to complete the inner section individually before using paired discussion to work on the more challenging outer section.

Bonus idea ★

For a real challenge, try removing the attribution at the bottom of a source and asking students to try and figure out who wrote it and when. This makes an engaging starter for a source-based lesson.

COP is simply a rubric for source analysis, in which you ask students to look at the **c**ontent, **o**rigin, and **p**urpose of a source. It's a memorable and analytical way of approaching sources and can be used independently of the COP board.

When using the COP board, students record the content, origin and purpose of the source in the appropriate section of an *inner* ring. In the outer circle they write the *implications* of what they have recorded for the question they are answering or enquiry they are undertaking. This is the challenging part, in which students think about reliability and usefulness.

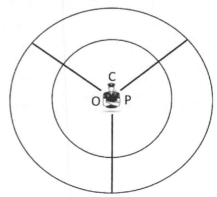

Source relay

'Over to you.'

Source relay — the creation of Carol Stobbs (@littlestobbsy) — is a fantastic task: collaborative, active and challenging. Students generate questions around a source before swapping sources and answering each other's questions.

Put students into pairs and allocate each pair a card or piece of paper with a different source on it. Get them to stick this source in the middle of a large blank piece of paper.

Students should think about the questions that an historian would ask in order to really understand the source. Give them a fixed amount of time to generate questions relating to its content, origin and purpose.

Students should write or stick their questions in the blank space around the source.

After a set period of time, ring a bell (or give some other kind of signal) to indicate that students should now pass their source to a different pair who will attempt to answer the questions over the course of the lesson.

Finally, the sources should be returned to their original owners, who should review the responses and decide whether anything remains unanswered.

Teaching tip

For those who need a bit more structure, provide question starter words (*who, what, when, where, why* and *how*) and ask them to form at least one question using each of these.

Bonus idea

@littlestobby's version contains a fuller question-generation matrix (by @johnsayers). You can view an excellent example at https://littlestobbsy.wordpress.com/2015/04/14/home-front-source-relay/.

One, two, three, four ... source analysis

'Four people, four sources.'

Katie Thoburn's four-part source analysis activity encourages students to practise, through lively discussion, the processes of cross-referencing and comparing sources.

Teaching tip

Differentiate this activity by thinking carefully about how you allocate sources within each group.

Display a source-based question that requires students to look at a set of sources and come to a judgement or conclusion. For example:

'How far do the sources suggest that the Battle of the Somme was a success for the British Army?'

Put students into groups of four and give each student a different source on the subject.

Step one: Give students *one* minute to quietly read or look at their allocated source, without writing anything down.

Step two: Give students *two* minutes to highlight significant sections or make any annotations.

Bonus idea ★

Once the students have planned their group answer, ask them to work independently to write it up, ideally as homework. They can then peer-mark it at the start of the following lesson.

Step three: Give students *three* minutes each to talk to the other students in the group, explaining their own source and listening to others explain theirs.

Step four: As a group, students have *four* minutes to collaboratively make a rough outline plan showing how they would tackle the question.

Look *harder!*

'Historical images offer windows into other worlds.'

The following activities are quick tricks to get students looking in greater detail at visual sources.

Pixelate it!: Pixelate or otherwise obscure key parts of an image and get students to speculate during paired conversation on what the pixels are concealing.

Describe and draw: Put the picture source in a concealed location (for example, on the back of the door). Divide the class into teams, each containing one 'recorder' and two 'memorisers'. Teams must send their memorisers to look at the picture. Each gets a maximum of thirty seconds to commit it to memory before returning to relate it to the recorder. An easier version of this activity involves students working in pairs and sitting back-to-back, with one holding and describing the source, and the other drawing what is described.

'It contains a cake and several men in suits': Tell students what the most important features of a picture are (and the subject matter being addressed) and ask them to sketch what it might look like; this works well as a starter in pairs when looking at political cartoons. This example is the famous cartoon on the Berlin Conference.

Concentric rings: Place a visual source in the middle of a larger sheet of paper, and draw three rings around it. Students make notes in the inner ring about what they can see, before using the outer rings to make observations or inferences of increasing complexity: what message the artist intended to convey, and finally *why* they might have sought to transmit this particular message.

Teaching tip

Visual sources make great materials for starters. See Idea 62: The mysterious picture starter.

Taking it further

In 'Describe and draw', get teams to swap their drawings, before projecting the original and asking students to mark one another's efforts.

Bonus idea ★

When you show students a visual source, introduce a delay before providing the explanatory caption, and ask them to make informed guesses about what it might say.

Jump into the picture

'Think Dick Van Dyke and that scene in Mary Poppins.'

Get students thinking about the thoughts and feelings of the people in an historical image by asking them to 'jump into' the scene.

Teaching tip

Provide students with images you are going to study in advance of the lesson, and ask them to complete the 'all five senses' task as homework. Assign different images to different students and then ask them to share their responses during the starter of the following lesson.

All five senses

This is a great activity to get students engaging with particularly evocative images like Hogarth's *Gin Lane* or action shots such as those of First World War soldiers crossing no-man's land. Students simply stick the image in the centre of the page and draw five boxes around the outside. Imagining that they are one of the people pictured (they choose which), they should write down what they can see, hear, smell, taste and feel, using one box per sense.

Thought bubbles/speech bubbles

Ask students to add speech bubbles to images, speculating about what the people pictured might be saying. Then, ask them to add thought bubbles to show what the same people might actually be thinking. This works well with photographs (what might the 'Big Three' have been saying to each other while having their picture taken at Yalta, and how might this have differed from their private thoughts?), or with cartoons (what might Pitt and Napoleon have been saying and thinking in the famous Gillray cartoon?).

Bonus idea ★

Try an app like Balloon Stickies to add speech or thought bubbles ready for students to fill.

Destroy that source!

'Scribble on it; cut it up; pull it to pieces ...'

Students should be encouraged to interact with sources — and this means making a mess of them.

a. Cut it up

Carol Stobbs's fantastic 'destroy a source' activity sees students deconstructing historical evidence in the most literal sense.

Provide each individual or pair with scissors, glue and a copy of the source you are examining. This works particularly well with visual sources, but it is possible to do it with written sources. Students should spend a few minutes looking at the source and deciding which aspects of it are the most important. They then cut these excerpts out and stick them down, leaving lots of blank space between them for annotations.

b. Scribble on it!

Get students used to reading sources in an active manner; annotating, circling and generally scribbling as they go.

- Project sources onto the whiteboard and model the annotation process during class discussion, or have students come to the front and make the annotations for you.
- Provide students with coloured highlighters when teaching them to cross-reference sources. They might, for example, use one colour to highlight bits of the source offering evidence in support of a statement, and another colour to highlight those which oppose it.
- Word-processors enable easy source annotation, allowing students to highlight sections and to insert comments.

> **Teaching tip**
>
> I collect up source inserts after exams and use the thoroughly annotated ones as examples in lessons.

> **Bonus idea** ★
>
> Ask students to rifle through each other's 'rubbish' (the discarded bits of the source) and find one thing which their partner should consider salvaging.

Skip diving for 'rubbish' sources

'A biased source is not a bad one.'

The word 'bias' can become the bane of the history teacher's life: students are quick to write off biased sources as though they have nothing at all to offer. In this activity, students take sources out of a bin bag, consider why someone might have put them there and then explain why they should be salvaged.

Taking it further

Equip students with a more sophisticated vocabulary for source analysis. Encourage them to talk about 'subjectivity' and 'vested interest' rather than bias, a word which has more negative connotations. Ask students to consider whether any account can ever be objective, and the implications of this for historians.

This activity is all about demonstrating to students that a source's usefulness and reliability depends on what you are trying to find out about. If you are studying life in Nazi Germany, you might look at an anti-Semitic propaganda poster. It does not offer a reliable image of the role of Jews in German society, but it does offer a useful insight into the motivations and methods of Nazi propagandists.

Put students into pairs or small groups and give each a bin bag containing between four and six sources on the topic or period being studied.

Provide them with a table in which to capture their ideas as they take each source out of the bin. The table should ask them to record:

- A description of the source
- Who wrote it and when
- A brief summary of what the source says
- Their thoughts on why the source might have been deemed useless
- Ideas about what the source *can* tell us.

The selfie portrait

'Selfies are a fixture of modern life. Just like historical portraits, they are heavy with symbolism.'

We want students to understand that portraits are carefully composed images conveying layered messages about the sitter's identity. To illustrate this, ask students to construct and take their own 'selfie portraits' and to analyse each other's.

Think of the Rainbow Portrait of Elizabeth I. Such complex portraits require detailed analysis. Our students know more than they realise, however, about symbolic portraiture: they compose images of themselves all the time, publishing them online.

- Introduce students to an historical portrait and ask them what messages it conveys about the sitter. A good way to do this is by making notes around the image in concentric rings, as suggested in Idea 19: Look *harder!*. You will need to help students access the messages they are likely to miss.
- Set a homework task in which students compose their own 'selfie portraits'. They should aim to tell us as much about themselves and their values as possible without using any words.
- You can make this more challenging by asking them to imagine that they are standing for Student Council. How might they tailor their selfie-portrait to account for this situation?
- At the start of the next lesson, ask students to analyse each other's portraits in exactly the same way as they analysed the historical portrait in the previous lesson.
- Now ask students to have another go at analysing an historical portrait. Are they able to do so more critically?

Teaching tip

Self-conscious students may be uncomfortable with taking photographs of themselves and some prefer to paint or draw their selfie portraits instead. This makes for an excellent cross-curricular project with the art department.

Half and half

'When two halves make a funny-looking whole.'

Another credit to Carol Stobbs here (@littlestobbsy) for this activity, guaranteed to get students really engaging with visual sources.

Taking it further

Get students annotating the image – both the side originally provided and the side they create. Annotating the original side before they move on to working on their own drawing is important in helping them to think about what has been included and, more importantly, what has been left out.

Take a picture source – such as a portrait, a political cartoon or a propaganda piece – and cut it in half. Provide students with one half only. They must stick the half picture down and then complete it by drawing the other half. There are various ways of doing this:

Using a written source: For example, when looking at portraits, provide them with a less flattering contemporary account of what the sitter looked like. When looking at someone like Elizabeth I, this may produce two very contrasting halves.

Using various sources and their learning to offer a more balanced picture: For example, when looking at the 1887 commemorative Empire Plate which celebrates the British Empire, have students create an alternative half of the plate, offering a more negative interpretation of the Empire's impact.

Using their learning to make informed guesses: Having studied the Treaty of Versailles, for example, students are provided with half a political cartoon on that topic and must use their imaginations – and knowledge of the period – to complete it. Think of the cartoon in which Germany is portrayed as a condemned man approaching a guillotine. If you crop Clemenceau and Wilson out of the picture, can your students work out who is missing and what they might be doing?

Using objects as sources

'What do the contents of your pencil case say about you?'

All relics tell stories; some tell complex and controversial ones. Students should be encouraged to look at relics or artefacts with the same curiosity and criticality they would bring to bear when using written sources.

An appreciation of the role of non-written sources in the piecing together of history is important, particularly when it comes to addressing our tendency to see literacy as the marker of civilisation and to prioritise the study of literate over pre-literate societies. Here are a few ways of incorporating relic and artefact analysis into your classroom practice:

Look for deliberate narratives: Ask students to think about how man-made objects have been used to convey stories. Coins have always been used to carry non-written messages about states or rulers to wide audiences. Get students to inspect the coins in their pockets and discuss whether this is still the case.

Look for non-deliberate clues: Skeletons, for example, can tell us a huge amount about how people lived and died, and students like speculating on how.

The mystery object: Bring in some of the mundane trappings of everyday life (the lid of a disposable coffee cup, for example) and ask students to imagine that these items are found ten thousand years from now. How might the archaeologists of the future figure out what they are and what guesses might they make about their uses?

The pencil case task: Get students investigating the contents of their partner's pencil case to make broader inferences about its owner.

> **Teaching tip**
>
> Museums from across the world post pictures of obscure artefacts on Twitter and invite the public to guess what they are. Search #mysteryobject to pick out a good one before you start the lesson.

> **Bonus idea**
>
> Some museums, libraries and local authorities lend boxes of artefacts to teachers for use in the classroom. If there's no such provision in your area, www.historyboxes.com is a small company which hires out boxes of artefacts – and will deliver.

Working with cartoons, satire and caricature

'We history teachers owe a lot to the cartoonists of the past: they inadvertently created some of the best history teaching resources imaginable.'

Cartoons make great stimulus material: they are engaging, thought-provoking and can be analysed at many different levels.

Teaching tip

Cartoons often rely on symbolism and idiom, making them difficult for EAL students. If the message hinges on a phrase such as 'burning one's bridges' or 'crying over spilt milk', ensure that everyone is familiar with the meaning of the idiom. Similarly, bear in mind that symbolism of things like animals and colours varies across cultures.

But cartoons can also be complex and difficult to interpret, relying on contextual knowledge and some understanding of cartoonists' techniques. We need to actively teach students how to interpret political cartoons.

First, show students a broad range of political cartoons or satirical images in order to introduce them to common techniques including **symbolism**, **sizing** and **positioning**, **caricature**, **irony** and **personification**. A PowerPoint presentation with examples of cartoons using each of these techniques can be found on the accompanying webpage for this book (www.bloomsbury.com/100-ideas-secondary-history/).

Now home in on the cartoon you want students to interpret, getting them to follow a few simple steps.

Many of the activities already covered also offer ideal ways to analyse political cartoons in the classroom:

- Get students looking properly at the image from the outset by not revealing the entire thing at once (see Idea 24: Half and half and Idea 19: Look *harder*!). Try removing faces of key figures, speech bubbles, captions and labels.

- Force them to make inferences about the origin by blanking out the attribution (Idea 16: Call the COP).
- Get them to isolate the most significant parts of the image through Idea 21: Destroy that source!
- Project a cartoon onto the whiteboard and annotate it collaboratively.

CARTOON ANALYSIS, STEP BY STEP	
Look briefly	Broadly speaking, what is the cartoon about?
Think about context	What do we already know about this topic? What different opinions about the topic might have existed at the time?
Look in detail	List the things you can see in the picture.
Identify techniques	Are any of the things you have listed symbolic? If so, how? Other than symbolism, which of the following persuasive techniques are used by the cartoonist? (Circle all you think apply) **Sizing – exaggeration – irony – caricature – positioning – personification**
Infer meaning	What does the cartoonist want viewers to take from the cartoon? (I.e. what is his or her message?)
Determine purpose	Why might the cartoonist have sought to convey this message?

Bonus idea ★

Russel Tarr suggests getting students to produce 'visual essays': compositions of multiple cartoons on a particular topic, grouped and analysed on poster paper so as to help answer an essay question, such as 'Describe how the Treaty of Versailles weakened Germany'. See www.classtools.net/blog/visual-essay-writing-cartoons-sticky-notes-and-plenty-of-collaboration/ for examples of what this looks like.

Find political cartoons online at:

http://www.punch.co.uk/gallery-list

https://archive.cartoons.ac.uk/

www.loc.gov/teachers/classroommaterials/primarysourcesets/political-cartoons/

Police investigations

'To be able to take a hypothesis apart, you need to know how one is put together.'

Police investigations are a neat way of promoting criticality in evidence handling and of illustrating the fact that there are often multiple and conflicting accounts of the same event. Provide students with a folder of sources about historical 'crimes' and ask them to construct and defend their own evidence-based interpretations of what occurred.

Teaching tip

'Hook' students by chalking an outline onto the floor or putting tape over the door to create a crime scene. Ask a colleague to pop in at the end of the lesson to play the returning superintendent and listen to the students' theories.

Taking it further

Get students to elaborate on and defend their interpretations by following your police investigation lesson with a court case (Idea 32: Historical figures on trial).

This lesson works well when investigating murders (think Kirov or the Princes in the Tower) and other historical crimes, such as Mary Queen of Scots' alleged treachery.

Students come into the classroom to find evidence folders marked 'TOP SECRET' on their desks, and a memo from their 'superintendent'.

The memo explains that there has been an incident and the superintendent wants his or her officers (the students) to investigate, come up with a theory based on the contents of the evidence folder and be ready to explain and defend this theory to him/her by the time he/she arrives back at the station (at the end of the lesson).

The students should work out what crime is supposed to have been committed and who the possible suspects are, as well as looking in detail at each piece of evidence. An information capture table with the following headings can be helpful.

Evidence code	Description	Who made it and why?	What does it suggest?	Your assessment of its usefulness to this investigation

Opposing *Wikipedia* entries

'This article has multiple issues. Please help improve it.'

Ask students to produce one-sided *Wikipedia* entries before swapping and reviewing each other's.

This idea, a simple but effective way to get students reading critically, comes from a training session run by Neil Smith, and is a staple in my classroom.

Divide the class into two. One half will produce *Wikipedia* articles that deliberately portray an event or development from a certain angle, while the other half will produce articles from the opposing stance.

Ideally, students produce their articles as homework. The following lesson, ask them to pair up with someone with a contrasting article. It's a good idea to have a few you have made earlier in your back pocket, unless you have a class of angels who always bring their homework in on time.

Students annotate their partners' work to show why it is an unfair representation of events.

Before they begin, discuss with students the kind of flaws they should look for in their partner's articles. This is a good way of getting them thinking about the habits of critical reading. You may decide, for example, that the most important flaws in any piece of historical writing are lack of evidence, lack of explanation and omission of detail.

You can really go to town with the *Wikipedia* analogy if you think your students will get on board. Instead of merely annotating their partner's article, they can mark it with the tags used by real 'Wikipedians', such as 'citation needed'.

Teaching tip

Not only is this a good way of practising critical reading, it also offers an ideal route into a discussion about the benefits and pitfalls of using *Wikipedia* as a source.

Making memorials

'Who decides how we should remember a particular aspect of the past — which facts to present and whose stories to tell?'

Inspired by the brilliant www.facinghistory.org, this task sees students examining the nature and purpose of memorials before creating their own memorial for the event(s) they are studying.

Taking it further

Introduce students to the concept of a 'counter-monument', a term that has been used to describe a number of Holocaust memorials and the 9/11 Memorial. Counter-monuments do not, in theory, offer interpretations or narratives, providing contemplation spaces instead. What are the advantages and disadvantages of this form of memorial?

Start with three minutes of small-group discussion, asking students to jot down points in response to the question, what's the point of a memorial? Ask pairs to feed their ideas back to the class. The ensuing discussion may touch upon issues from communal grief to social enforcement or propaganda. Push students' thinking by asking, are memorials always sad? Record ideas on the whiteboard.

Introduce students to various memorials (offering different perspectives, or from different times or places) to the events you are studying. First, give each small group a picture of, and information about, **one** of the memorials (for example, if you are studying the Battle of the Somme, one group might look at Jeremy Deller's recent, interactive #wearehere memorial while another looks at Thiepval Memorial). After five minutes, ask each group to feed back. Use targeted questioning to elicit students' views on the message and purpose of each memorial, referring back to the results of your initial discussion about the point of memorials.

Now provide everyone with small pictures of **all** of the monuments discussed. Ask them to stick them down and annotate them, creating a visual essay that examines the changing ways in which the event has been memorialised.

Finally, ask students to design a memorial that represents their own take on the event, based on everything they have learnt about it.

Carousel interpretation tasks

'Pass it on!'

This task allows students to look at a series of historical interpretations on the issue you are studying, considering the evidence supporting and contradicting each.

Carousel activities are an easy way to bring a bit of dynamism to a task. The 'carousel' bit simply refers to the fact that there is movement – either of the students or of the resources – so that groups or pairs have a finite chunk of time with each resource (this tends to focus and motivate them).

First, take four or five historians' interpretations of a topic, event or issue and strip them down to the bare bones. Write each summarised interpretation in the centre of a big piece of sugar paper. Leave plenty of space around it.

In a carousel interpretation task about the Norman Conquest, one of your papers might say 'Peter Rex (2009) argued that the Norman regime was built on brutality and deceitful propaganda'.

Put each interpretation on a different table. Students in small groups must use two colours of sticky notes to write down evidence in support of and against the interpretation, aiming to record at least two points on each side before their time at that table elapses. After about five minutes, groups move on to the next table and the next interpretation, leaving their sticky notes behind.

The activity becomes increasingly challenging with each round, as students have to read the points made by other groups and try to think of new ones.

Teaching tip

This task is impossible unless students have already accumulated strong subject knowledge. For this reason it needs to come fairly late on in a unit, or as a follow-up to a content-orientated homework task.

Taking it further

To make a whole lesson of this, get the students summarising the interpretations themselves (one per group or pair) before beginning the carousel. Book reviews offer short, accessible summaries of historians' arguments (see Idea 82: Making history books accessible).

Making debates work in the history classroom

'Holding a debate in a lesson sounds easy, so why do mine always fall flat?'

Debates require a lot of structure and preparation. The tried and tested formula below helps students get ready for a debate. It is based on recommendations from the fantastic www.noisyclassroom.com.

Teaching tip

Students who are very uncomfortable speaking in front of others may prefer to take on the role of note-takers for their team.

It's difficult to conduct a single debate with a group of thirty. Instead, be prepared to run *two* related debates with large classes. You will need a whole lesson for students to work in their teams preparing their points, and a second lesson in which to hold the debate.

The preparation lesson can be organised as follows.

Stage 1: brainstorming

Divide the class into four groups, giving each of these groups one side of one of the debate topics to prepare.

Give every member of the class a bunch of sticky notes and give individuals five minutes of silent time to write down their ideas, one per note.

The group members should then come together for a brainstorming session. They will need a large piece of paper and a group leader who will elicit each of the ideas from individuals and stick the corresponding sticky notes onto the paper, with duplicate ideas being stuck together.

Stage 2: organising ideas

The group leader takes another large piece of paper and writes 1-9 down the side. Together, students identify seven to nine main arguments from the brainstorming stage, joining similar ideas together and getting rid of less powerful ones. They should give each of their arguments a short name, about three words long.

Groups should then divide themselves up, allocating the following roles:

- **Speakers:** Ideally, each speaker takes around three points.
- **Summariser:** This person will speak once all the points have been made, rounding up the argument.
- **Timekeeper or Chair.**

Stage 3: structuring speeches

Explain that each point will require a short, structured speech, and that speeches should include the following:

- An **introduction:** stating the thrust of the team's argument.
- A **preview**: giving the names of the points the individual speaker will cover.
- A **rebuttal**: a brief statement of why the previous speaker's points should be disregarded.
- **Points:** for each, the speaker should use the PEE structure, naming the **point, explaining** the reasoning and giving key **evidence** for the point. They should make only minimal notes, to ensure that the debate itself does not become an exercise in reading aloud.

Whilst the speakers are preparing their speeches:

Each group's summariser needs to decide what they think the biggest issues in the debate will be and prepare a brief speech focusing on those with which he or she will close the team's argument. The chairs, timekeepers and any other pupils should think about what the other side might say and come up with ideas to rebut them.

For ideas on running the debate itself go to http://noisyclassroom.com.

Bonus idea

For imaginative variations on the usual debate format, try www.classtools.net where Russel Tarr explains how to run 'boxing match' and 'balloon' debates.

Historical figures on trial

'King Richard, how do you plead?'

Teach students to put together water-tight and evidence-based arguments and to find flaws in opposing views by holding mock trials.

Teaching tip

Make clear that your judgements will be *modern* ones – the point of this exercise is not to create a mock-up historical courtroom. Doing so would require students to have impossible insights into the minds and morals of people from the past!

Taking it further

Unlike the police investigation activity, the trial activity requires students to start with a premise about what happened and who was responsible, and then to build a case to support this. This raises important questions about historians and their processes. While some, including Geoffrey Elton, argued that historians should be led by evidence, approaching it without predetermined questions in mind, others see this as unrealistic and believe that historians will inevitably bring presuppositions to their investigations. What do your students think?

Put individuals, groups, and even whole nations on trial when assessing their contributions to or responsibility for events or developments. You might look at 'real' crimes (perhaps as a follow-up to the police investigation lesson), or try people for particular interpretations of their actions. Was Haig guilty of gross-incompetence? Was the British Empire guilty of stifling progress in its colonies?

The key to making this activity work is giving students adequate preparation time and very clear instructions. Allocate the following roles:

- A defendant
- A barrister for the defence
- Witnesses for the defence
- A barrister for the prosecution
- Witnesses for the prosecution.

In large classes, simply dividing the class into a defence and a prosecution team would leave you with excessively large groups. In this case, consider running two related but different trials, so that you can divide the class into four groups instead. While two of the teams go head-to-head in the first trial, the other two act as court reporters and members of the jury, before everyone swaps roles for the second trial.

Ask students to produce reports (newspaper reports work well here) at the end of the lesson or as homework, summarising the cases made, the key evidence in support of each, and the decision of the jury.

On Tuesday 13 January, 1671, a flea farted. Is this history?

'This made my brain hurt – in a good way.' (Mus, 16)

Looking at the difference between 'everything that's ever happened' and 'history', this diagram asks students to consider when and how the past becomes history.

Draw a giant circle on the board and label it 'everything that has ever happened'. Inside it, at the very centre, draw a tiny circle labelled 'historians' output'. Ask students to think about why the second circle is so much smaller than the first.

Now add concentric circles between the two that you have drawn, so that you end up with a diagram that looks like an archery target. Your biggest circle is 'everything that ever happened'. Within it, decreasing in size with each stage are circles labelled as follows:

- Experienced
- Recorded
- Records available
- Accessed by historians
- Used to inform historians' output
- Historians' output.

See the resource on this book's accompanying web page for the resultant diagram (www.bloomsbury.com/100-ideas-secondary-history/). The diagram represents the process by which the past is transformed into history, and each step presents opportunities for important discussion. How does each stage play a role in shaping history?

Home in on the final stage in which historians interpret their chosen sources and use them to build written histories, probing students' understanding of what else comes into play here to shape the historian's output.

Teaching tip

Before beginning this activity, ask students what they think history is. Many will reply with something along the lines of 'things that happened in the past'. We need to move them away from this preconception, towards a place where they engage critically with history and the processes behind it.

Taking it further

Refer sixth-form students to E.H. Carr's short work, *What is History?* It's worth keeping a copy in your classroom.

Mini-debates

'Effective, inclusive and ridiculously easy to organise.'

Quicker and easier to run than traditional debates, mini-debates are just as good at getting students talking about historical issues from different perspectives. Students work in groups of three made up of two debaters and a recorder. This idea comes from Dave Elston.

Teaching tip

Person C can also act as a referee, ensuring person A and B get five minutes each in which to make their points.

Suppose you are examining the statement, 'The US was right to drop atomic bombs on Japan in 1945.' Firstly, split the class into three groups: A, B and C. People in Group A will be defending the statement, Group B will be arguing against it and Group C will be tasked with recording and presenting the points. Group C should include those students requiring most support.

Preparation:

- Groups A and B, in private, should talk through the issues before individually noting down what they *personally* think are the three strongest points.
- With Group C, talk through the kinds of arguments that might come up on both sides and how these arguments could be challenged. Provide these students with information capture sheets or grids for the next stage (see online resources).

The debates:

- Split the main groups up into separate groups of three, including one representative from each group.
- For ten minutes, the person from A and B go head-to-head in a mini-debate while person C uses the grid provided earlier to note down both debaters' arguments.

Feedback:

- Stop the mini-debates and call the class to order.
- Allow fifteen minutes or so for feedback. During this time, call upon each group's recorder (person C) to report back on the points made in their particular mini-debate.
- As these ideas are fed back to you, insert them into a master list or grid on the whiteboard. Members of the original Group C can simply add new ideas to those already in their grids while others make notes on each side of the debate.
- By the end of the lesson, everyone has a record of all the arguments made, on both sides of the debate, by *all* of the debaters.

Taking it further

For homework, ask students to write a balanced response that reaches a considered judgement. They should use the notes they made during the debate feedback session as the basis for this.

The history vs. story Venn diagram

'What is history but a fable agreed upon?'

If Napoleon really wanted an answer to this question he should have had a go at this activity, the brainchild of Richard Kennett (@kenradical). Ideal for sixth-formers or able GCSE students, it encourages students to think about the nature of the discipline.

Taking it further

Instead of a Venn diagram, try a spectrum or gradient. This allows for more nuanced discussion.

Draw a large Venn diagram, such as the one illustrated below – you can do this on the board, or pairs can do it on mini-whiteboards.

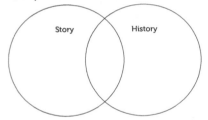

Discuss the difference between histories and stories, and see how many points the students come up with independently.

Then provide them with this jumbled list and see where they position each point. NB There is no single correct version of this!

- Constructed by whoever is doing the telling
- May be fictional
- Purpose is usually to entertain
- Compiled by investigation and study
- Always relates to the past
- Based on evidence
- Purpose is usually to inform and educate
- Routinely challenged
- A form of artistic expression
- May be used for political purposes
- Contributes to communal identity.

Creative and imaginative tasks

Part 3

Ways with role play

'I keep a few old ties and a couple of pairs of glasses in my drawer.'

Role playing offers students opportunities to look at historical motivation, helping explain why people in the past behaved as they did.

Teaching tip

It really is worth buying some cheap dressing-up accessories – moustaches; monocles; capes; plastic crowns, and so on. It's surprising how much of an effect they have on students' involvement in role play.

Taking it further

People who committed horrific or otherwise incomprehensible acts centuries ago were not usually evil, stupid or insane; they were acting in ways that seemed rational to them at the time. If we agree that rationality is relative, can we ever hope to fully understand the motives, values and concerns of people in the past? What are the implications of this, both for this task and for the study of history more generally?

There are lots of fun and thought-provoking activities centred around role play. These are just a few of my favourites.

Facing the press

When modern politicians face the press, they anticipate questions and prepare answers. Similarly, journalists prepare their questions. In this activity, students play historical figures, spin doctors and journalists, and have plenty of preparation time before they pose or answer any questions.

Put students into groups of six, which should then split into two teams of three. One team will consist of the historical figure in question and two spin doctors; the other team will consist of three journalists.

Give students ten to fifteen minutes to prepare. The historical figure and spin doctors should think about which issues the journalists are likely to home in on, and how best to answer related questions, while the journalists must think about which topics the historical figure will be trying to dodge and how they will force him or her to confront them.

Conferences and meetings

Ask students to run a village hall or community meeting, in which local people air their concerns about the issues affecting their lives. By varying their roles, you encourage them to think about the ways in which people of different ages, genders and occupations were affected.

Peace conferences make good subject material for role play. Ask different students to represent different combatant groups, thinking carefully about what they want to get out of a settlement and what bargaining tools they might use in the negotiations before role playing the conference itself. I usually do this with students when looking at the Treaty of Versailles.

The society in miniature – attributing roles to a whole class

At the start of a unit, think about the groups whose experiences you want students to understand. Give every student in the class a role as a member of one of these groups. Students should get to know the person they represent. This can be a fun homework task – most enjoy choosing a name and a picture. Once they have created the characters, use them in role play scenarios, or simply in class discussion. Encourage students to get into the habit of asking, 'How does this affect my character?' and comparing their answers with those of their classmates.

> **Bonus idea**
>
> Role play activities fail when young people feel uncomfortable. Think about what your students will be comfortable with, and build up gradually to asking them to do anything that requires an element of performance.

The historical action figure

'The crusader knight action figure is now 30% more pious! Bonus features include large private retinue!'

Get students thinking about the defining features of historical individuals or roles by designing the packaging for action figures.

Teaching tip

Do the thinking and planning in class time and get students to create the finished packaging at home, either on computers or by hand.

Taking it further

For more ideas and a template, see the great example on Quinn Rollins's website: www.quinnrollins.com/p/templates.html

This activity is great fun. There are two ways of using it.

1) To look at a role

What defines the ideal medieval king or perfect wartime president? Students should think about the features, accessories and abilities that the perfect candidate would possess and then design the corresponding action figure, signposting his or her attributes on the packaging. *'Includes glorious war record!'*

2) To look at an individual

Students create the packaging for the figurine of a specific individual in order to home in on key aspects of his or her historical role (see the example below).

RICHARD NIXON
ACTION FIGURINE

FREE bonus features include:

Office recoding system!

Plane ticket to China

$19.99 NOW: $0.99

Now also available:

Haldeman
Ehrlichman
Kissinger

Collect the set!

Pull the string to hear him say 'I am not a crook!'

BEST BEFORE: 09.08.74
Batteries not included

Students as cartoonists

'The best way to understand the cartoonist's art is to have a go at it.'

Not only do students tend to thoroughly enjoy it, designing political cartoons is an excellent way of exploring interpretation and promotes the critical viewing skills they need to independently interpret historical cartoons.

Was Henry's attack on the monasteries prompted by monastic corruption or by his own greed? Were the Suffragettes publicity-hungry terrorists or brave activists? How better to explore debates like these than through cartoons?

Having studied an event or development and the various ways that people at the time reacted to it, ask students to design cartoons depicting it from a specific stance. You can let them choose the message they wish to convey, or split the class in half and get them presenting different standpoints.

Another approach is to provide students with a genuine historical cartoon that presents a particular stance on an issue, and ask them to produce one presenting the opposing stance.

Make sure your students are aware of the various techniques cartoonists use to convey their messages, including sizing, analogy and caricature (see www.bloomsbury.com/100-ideas-secondary-history). An excellent worksheet, created by Russel Tarr, is available at www.classtools.net/blog/design-a-cartoon/ and gets students thinking about how to use symbolism and idiom in their cartoons.

Teaching tip

Cartoon design activities such as this one are an ideal follow-up to activities that require students to analyse real political cartoons (see Idea 26: Working with cartoons, satire and caricature).

Bonus idea ★

Cartoon design is distinct from storyboarding, which involves students transposing a narrative into pictures. For an effective homework task, ask students to create a storyboard around an historical event or development – this will help reinforce their chronological knowledge. (See Idea 87: Creative technology.)

Decision-making tasks

'Decision-making activities are an excellent way for pupils to investigate the complexity of human motivation and address the fallacy of causal inevitability.' (Andy Harmsworth)

Ask students to look at historical situations through the eyes of the people involved to try to understand the decisions they made.

Teaching tip

Initiate a discussion about the difficulties of trying to place ourselves in the shoes, or rather the minds, of people living centuries ago. Does contextual difference make this so difficult that it is not worth trying? See the 'Taking it Further' section of Idea 36: Ways with role play.

The following outline for how to run a decision-making activity is based on the advice of history teacher Andy Harmsworth, the Schools History Project regional adviser for the South East.

- Isolate a key question involving a decision taken by the individual or group you are studying. You can either provide the question or let students help shape it. Phrase it in the present tense: 'It is 1916. Should Irish republicans start an armed uprising against the British?'.
- Groups should brainstorm what they already know about the context in order to identify constraints and considerations.
- Lay out the various courses of action the decision-makers could follow. Again, you can either provide students with a pre-prepared list or thrash one out through class discussion.
- Groups should discuss the advantages and disadvantages of each course of action before choosing one. It can be fun to do this as a meeting between historical figures (see Idea 36: Ways with role play).
- Students should feed back on their decisions, explaining their reasoning.
- Then reveal to pupils the decision that was actually taken. Groups should compare it with their chosen course of action and discuss the reasons for any differences.

Taking it further

Having looked at the chief consequences of the decision actually taken, students can discuss which were intended and which were unintended, and whether the consequences justify the decision.

The chocolate game

'Just remember to share the chocolates out when it's all over ...'

This exercise is perfect for examining the mechanisms of historical power struggles and, unsurprisingly, it's always popular.

Put students into groups, and ask them to assume the roles of various characters involved in the particular power struggle you are looking at. Give the group a set number of chocolates, and ask them to divvy them up in such a way that represents the power of each member of the group at the start of the power struggle.

You will then reveal, at intervals, historical developments affecting the power struggle. For example 'X dies', 'Y forms an alliance with Z'. There are various ways of doing this. You can simply announce a development every couple of minutes, flash a headline up on the board, or hand out newspaper clippings. See www.fodey. com for a great newspaper clipping generator.

Each time they learn of a new development, the group must consider how the unfolding events help shift power (or in this case chocolates) from one faction or individual to another. They should make a collective decision and then reallocate the chocolates accordingly.

When the activity is over, use whole-class discussion to check students' understanding. You can then ask them write up a summary of the power struggle.

Teaching tip

It helps if you ask students to record the way that power shifts in response to developments by noting this down in a table (see www.bloomsbury. com/100-ideas-secondary-history).

Bonus idea ★

Ask students to write up their summaries in the form of live news feeds to give the sense of the story unfolding.

Historical top trumps

'Trotsky scores well on military credentials but Stalin pips him on political cunning ...'

Ask students to make considered comparisons of historical figures by creating sets of top trumps cards.

Teaching tip

Combining this idea with Idea 53: Character cards is a fun way to create a set of resources that will prove useful over the course of the unit and as a revision aid.

This task works particularly well when you are studying an historical power struggle (comparing Lenin's would-be successors and asking why Stalin prevailed) or when looking at how well different figures performed in a certain role (comparing the legacies of a range of US presidents).

Students should produce a card for each of the individuals being compared. This requires them to think about the necessary attributes for the role in question and consider each of the figures in relation to these.

Looking at the 1066 contest for the English crown, pupils might decide that contenders needed a strong claim to the throne; experience of leadership; access to resources and military prowess. They would score each contender on each of these criteria. If you are looking at a sufficiently large set of individuals, students will actually be able to use the cards they have made to play the game at the end of the lesson.

The pitfall of activities like this is that students spend ages producing something that looks pretty, but skim over the bit where they have to do the historical thinking. To avoid this happening, ask them to print out the pictures they will need in advance of the lesson, or simply provide them with images and give them card templates to fill in.

Bonus idea ★

Make a class set of giant top trumps cards, dividing the class into small groups and assigning them one card to complete per group.

Do your worst!

'What would a *bad* one look like?'

This idea, from Mary Feerick, sees students producing 'dummy' chunks of historical writing, complete with the mistakes we want them to avoid.

How often do you come across students who make the same mistake again and again, apparently immune to your carefully-crafted feedback? My personal bugbears are sweeping generalisations and wishy-washy conclusions that fail to reach a judgement. This activity offers a creative way to promote good historical writing.

Having discussed the skill or skills you are trying to promote (for example, the use of appropriate and specific historical information to back up statements about the past), put students in pairs. Working together they should pen a few sentences or a paragraph that fails completely in this respect. Students can get quite into this – but doing it on a mini-whiteboard or on scrap paper underlines the point that this is a throw-away example, not something to spend too much time on.

Pairs can then swap examples, or, if you have a visualiser you can display and discuss a few. Students tend to get quite competitive about who has produced the worst piece of work! Move quickly on from this to the point of the exercise – getting them to produce strong piece of historical writing that successfully demonstrates the skill or characteristic you have been talking about.

Teaching tip

Paige Richardson uses this approach to promote behaviour for learning, asking new students (age 11-12) to demonstrate what someone who isn't listening looks like (they enjoy theatrically slouching and fidgeting) before asking them to demonstrate the opposite. It's then easy to ask students to get into the 'listening position' with a quick and gentle reminder, safe in the knowledge that they understand what is expected of them.

Taking it further

For more on encouraging students to reflect on their work, see Idea 71: Peer and self-marking techniques for the history classroom.

Get trading

'But why can't the government just print more money?'

Historical trading games involve students being allocated 'money' to demonstrate historical economic scenarios: in these examples, stock market bubbles and hyper-inflation.

Demonstrate inflation with a class auction.

- Put students into four teams. Allocate ten tokens to each team.
- Select seven classroom objects (board-rubbers, staplers, pens) to be the 'lots'. You can change the number of teams, but to make the activity work, you'll need more lots than teams.
- Hold an auction for each lot. As each is sold, record the price it fetched on the board.
- The winning team is the one that buys the most lots.

In the second round, illustrate price inflation by increasing the number of tokens but keeping the lots the same, so that more currency is chasing the same goods:

- Double the tokens allocated to each team. Repeat the whole process. This time, students should see that the prices recorded on the board will be more (roughly double) what they were in the first round.

The classroom stock exchange

- Give all students Monopoly money or tokens.
- In round one, announce that you have set up a company. Offer the opportunity to buy shares.
- Flash up a headline about how well the economy – and your company – is doing. (See www.fodey.com for a clipping generator.)

Bonus idea ★

Economic history has a reputation for being dry – but introducing students to economic principles makes for penny-dropping moments galore as they grasp the fundamentals. Take it back to first principles by asking the question 'what is money?'

- Issue dividends in Monopoly money or tokens to those who bought shares.
- Repeat in a second round, but this time put the price of the shares – and the dividend – up. The demand should rise as students clamber for the lucrative shares.
- With each round, plot the share price on the board. Allow students to sell to one another between rounds, too.
- Begin to introduce less profitable rounds and negative headlines. What happens to demand now? Eventually, students will watch the stock market crash and find that they cannot shift their unprofitable shares, even for low prices.

Teaching tip

Neil MacGregor's History of the World in 100 Objects is available as a series of podcasts (http://www.bbc.co.uk/programmes/b00nrtd2/episodes/downloads). For the episodes relating to trade and money, go to http://www.bbc.co.uk/programmes/p0147wjj.

The advertising agency

'Make it catchy!'

Advertisement generation tasks offer pupils opportunities to show their understanding creatively.

Teaching tip

A good rule of thumb if you are going to ask students to draw is to get them planning in class and drawing at home. This means that class time is used most efficiently – for thinking and discussion.

Logos: Students come up with logos for historical organisations or developments. This is extremely useful when they have to remember lots of similar or related things – such as agencies of the New Deal or acts of the Reformation Parliament. It makes a good plenary when done on mini-whiteboards, with students having to determine what their partner's logos represent.

Modern coats of arms: These are essentially just personal logos. How much information about an historical figure's values and deeds can be recorded in a shield-shaped picture?

Public information campaigns: Get students generating the type of posters put out by governments to influence public behaviour during epidemics or wartime.

Colour supplement advertisements: Let students record the details of, for example, a cure for the Black Death or an historically-significant technological innovation such as the spinning jenny by making an advertisement for it in the style of the ads typically found in newspaper colour supplements.

Lonely hearts ads: These work well when looking at concepts of masculinity and femininity and the ideal husband or wife at various points in history.

Commemorative stamps: When you are looking at a series of individuals – for example, the presidents of the 1920s – have students make a set of stamps but ban images of people. What images will they choose to represent each figure?

Commemorative plates: Get a pack of plain paper plates and have students design commemorative plates for events studied. Better still, show them a real commemorative plate, (such as the 1887 'Empire Plate') and have them redesign it to offer a contrasting interpretation.

Slogans: If the essence of the Truman Doctrine or the purpose of the Domesday Book had to be encapsulated into a catchy and memorable advertising slogan, what would it be?

 Bonus idea

A nice prize for the best logo, stamp, plate or coat of arms is to photograph it and feature it on your school website or in the newsletter.

Shoebox exhibitions

'The best homework project, ever.' (Casey, 14)

Ask students to make miniature exhibitions by collecting (or creating) artefacts and documents that shed light upon a topic. While a shoebox makes an ideal vessel for a mini-exhibition, it's also easy to make a virtual version on the free online tool Padlet if you prefer.

Teaching tip

Allow time for students to look at each other's exhibitions and question the 'curators' about what they have chosen to include.

Taking it further

Ask students to think about what museums can tell us about the societies for which they are designed. The Great Exhibition of 1851 makes an excellent case study here. And what should we make of museums that present history in ways that are no longer acceptable? The controversy surrounding the Belgian Museum for Central Africa and its portrayal of Belgian colonial history provides food for thought.

In some cases, it may be possible for students to get their hands on real artefacts and documents for their exhibitions. If you are studying the recent history of the local area, for example, they may be able to make copies of documents from a local archive, or even to access family papers or photographs. In the vast majority of cases, though, it will be necessary for students to make use of their creative faculties, and many will enjoy making the exhibits.

An exhibition on American youth culture in the 1960s might include a flyer for an anti-war protest and a postcard home from Woodstock, while an exhibition on Norman colonisation might include a page from the Domesday Book and a map showing the locations of Anglo Saxon uprisings. Each exhibit should have a label attached, explaining what it tells us about the topic in question.

If your students would rather make virtual exhibitions, Padlet is a simple website allowing you to pin images, videos and sections of text to a digital 'wall' (see Idea 87: Creative technology, for more details).

The mind's eye

'The world is but a canvas to our imagination.' (Henry David Thoreau)

This activity is all about trying to get inside the minds of people in the past. Ask students to draw a large outline of a head and/or brain and, inside, to draw or write about the outlooks, dreams, hopes or fears of an individual or group of people from the period you are studying.

This works particularly well for looking at ideas that drove historical phenomena, such as the Red Scare or the American Dream. Students may base their drawings or phrases on their knowledge of the period, or you may provide them with written sources from which they can take information and inspiration. What might mind's-eye drawings of the following look like?

Teaching tip

Assign different 'minds' to different students to examine how various people from the same period viewed an issue or situation.

- The Germany envisaged by the Nazis
- The America imagined by poor European emigrants of the nineteenth century
- The world beyond Europe as imagined before the age of European exploration
- The Great Society as envisaged by Lyndon Johnson
- Hell as imagined by medieval peasants.

A similar activity involves taking an image – for example of European emigrants disembarking at Ellis Island – and adding illustrated or written thought bubbles to the people in the image. See Idea 20: Jump into the picture.

Bonus idea ★

Students can annotate their drawings to explain what is going on – and, in some cases draw what actually happened outside of the head to show the difference between what people expected and what actually happened.

Display and resources

Part 4

Classroom vs. corridor

'Use classroom walls to enable learning, and corridor walls to showcase it.'

Your classroom walls are a powerful and free resource. Use them to move the historical learning on while using display areas beyond the classroom to show off students' work and promote the study of history.

Teaching tip

Many teachers don't have the luxury of teaching in one classroom or even one area of the school. If your timetable sends you far and wide, consider negotiating small spaces for history displays.

Taking it furthe

Create displays at particular points in the year, including Black History Month, International Women's Day and Holocaust Memorial Day, to help keep history at the forefront of staff and students' minds.

Bonus idea ★

Some teachers on Twitter report using whiteboard markers to turn windows into innovative display features. Students also love writing on bedroom windows or mirrors for revision if parents will let them.

Classroom displays provide an opportunity to:

Help contextualise learning: Maps, timelines and images of key figures help students build a mental visual framework around their learning. See Idea 48: Active Timelines and Idea 50: Ways of using maps, for this.

Support students in their writing: Sentence starters, key spellings and writing prompts can be displayed around the room to aid writing development.

Encourage questioning: In addition to presenting challenging, abstract questions about history (Idea 49: Displaying big questions), display enquiry questions to help keep students focused.

Corridors and communal spaces offer an ideal opportunity to...

Showcase excellent work: Displaying exceptional student work is a good way to reward hard workers and encourage aspiration.

Publicise history: Displays that inform the viewer about what studying history at your school entails will be useful to students considering their options. They will also enlighten other staff on what goes on in your department, helping to sow the seeds for cross-curricular collaboration.

Active timelines

'Introducing a timeline to my classroom made explanation so much simpler.'

Make timelines not only a feature of your walls but a regular feature of your lessons, adding and referring to them as a matter of course.

Having timelines in your classroom not only builds students' sense of chronology; it also allows you to examine historical concepts such change over time and causal relationships between events. The 'active timeline' is a display feature, active because it may be altered, annotated or otherwise built into lessons.

Categorise different types of historical developments: Attach symbols to the timeline events to trace particular developments. For example, on a timeline of medicine through time, you could add a certain symbol to all events showing the changing role of government in public health. Or you could categorise events by colour, displaying, for example, social, economic and political developments on variously-coloured cards.

High and low points: Place event cards either above or below the timeline to denote their impact. On a timeline of the campaign for female suffrage, where would the Cat and Mouse Act go relative to the 1908 Women's Sunday march?

Simultaneous timelines: When looking at two chronologically simultaneous but geographically separate topics (perhaps as different units), display the timelines parallel to one another to prompt students to think about how events are connected.

Woven timelines: Use wool or string to show causal links between events.

Teaching tip

All of the timeline-based activities suggested here can be done collaboratively.

Taking it further

Ask students to produce individual active timelines as homework projects over the course of a unit. They should add to them after each lesson and show you evidence of how they are progressing before handing in their masterpieces at the end of the unit.

Bonus idea ★

Washing lines strung across the classroom make good active timelines. It's easy to peg extra things on as the unit progresses.

Displaying big questions

'All pupils stare off into space now and then. So stick something in that space to engage their brains.'

Use your classroom walls to display the questions that you want students to keep at the front of their minds, or questions to stretch their thinking during quiet moments.

Taking it further

Get your most able students into the habit of looking to the walls for their extension questions, choosing the more challenging, abstract questions and noting down or discussing their responses.

Enquiry questions: If your unit is built around an enquiry question, it is essential that all students know what it is and that you refer back to it regularly. Displaying it somewhere prominent helps ensure that it remains the focal point of the learning.

Past exam questions: GCSE and A-level students can be asked how they could use what they've just learnt to help them answer one or more of the questions displayed.

Moral and philosophical questions: Some topics raise poignant and controversial questions, such as 'should the nations that benefitted from the slave trade apologise to the descendants of the enslaved?'. It's interesting to look at whether students' responses change as their knowledge of the topic in question develops.

Questions about the nature of history: What is history? Is there any such thing as an historical fact? Displaying such questions is important, even if it simply shows students that such fundamentals are up for discussion.

Questions to prompt 'macro' historical thinking: This type of big question (why do empires rise, and what causes them to fall? What makes a great leader? How far can individuals shape historical change?), will really stretch your most able students and require them to make links between different aspects of their historical knowledge.

Bonus idea ★

Ask students to add sticky note responses to the questions on the wall.

Ways of using maps

'Human history is fundamentally shaped by geography.'

Maps — from world maps to those of the immediate area — make fantastic active display features. Use them in your lessons to demonstrate the many ways of thinking about space by adding annotation, stories and images.

Imagine trying to understand the fall of the Romanovs without understanding the vastness of Russia, or the spread of the Black Death without looking at the trade routes of the middle ages. Displaying maps not only helps give students a sense of place, it adds an extra dimension to the discussion of history.

A few ideas for activities with maps:

- Add pictures to maps so students can visualise landscapes and think about the impact they might have had on people and events. For example, stick photos of plains, deserts and mountains to maps of the routes taken by wagon trains of the Old West.
- Add markers to a map over the course of a unit or lesson to show chronological development. For example, when looking at the Peasants' Revolt, make marks on a map of England to show how it progressed. Use different symbols to signify different types of development.
- Point out natural and man-made features, and ask students to consider the impact of these upon historical developments. Port cities are often important in the spread of new ideas, while rivers and mountain ranges often mark national boundaries.
- Get some inflatable globes and have students mark out key locations with sticky dots, and migrations or trade routes with dry-wipe pens.
- Build virtual tours of historical journeys or locations (see Idea 88: Virtual historical tours).

Taking it further

Display a large map of the local area as a 'story catcher' and have visitors annotate it with memories or local stories at parents' evenings and open evenings.

Graffiti walls

'Kids are told as toddlers not to scribble on walls ... so they're hard-wired to want to do it as teenagers.'

Graffiti walls are becoming increasingly common in history classrooms. They allow students to prominently display their reactions to a topic, to raise questions and offer ideas. By allowing the wall to 'grow' over the course of a term you create a visual record of how learning has developed.

At the start of term, cover part of your wall with cheap lining or sugar paper and stock up on chunky marker pens. The graffiti wall is a place for students to air their ideas. Here are some ways to build it into lessons:

- Put the enquiry question at the centre and allow students to add information that helps answer it over the course of the unit.
- Let them add their own questions about the topic. Others may write answers, or students may find that they are able to revisit and answer their own questions as the term goes on.
- Make the graffiti wall part of a regular plenary task. For example, having done your 'tell it in ten' activity (Idea 61: Quick progress checks), collaboratively decide on the best sentence and then ask its author to write it on the wall.
- Ask students to present a piece of information as a doodle or a series of pictograms. You could assign different information to different students and discuss what each other's pictograms signify.

Taking it further

Create a graffiti wall for parents' evening and let the parents visiting your classroom add to it. You could start them off with something like 'my dream history curriculum would include ...'.

Bonus idea ★

Let students photograph sections of the wall on their phones to help them with revision or homework.

Using period and region-specific music to set the scene

'Music can transform the classroom atmosphere in an instant.'

Play music appropriate to the country and decade you are studying. This is incredibly easy to do thanks to the brilliant radiooooo.com.

Music in the history classroom can bring the subject matter to life. Radiooooo.com allows you to play music from the country and decade of your choice, going back to 1900. Transport students to 1920s Japan, 1940s France or 1960s Cuba while they work. For periods before the twentieth century, YouTube turns up excellent results. I love Gregorian chants for their concentration-boosting powers (though my students aren't as keen). These are just a few of the many ways to enrich your classroom environment with historical music.

- Play music as students enter the room to set the scene for the lesson to come.
- Play music during timed tasks, explaining that students will need to stop working on the task when the music stops.
- Use music to routinely indicate periods in which you expect students to be working independently and quietly.
- Use music to help students calm down or to re-energise the class. Radiooooo.com lets you specify whether you want fast or slow music.
- Play background music during role-play tasks (see Idea 36: Ways with role play). This works particularly well with the cocktail party and speed dating activities.

Taking it further

Get dancing! Why not have a go at the popular dances of the period you are studying? There are YouTube videos that will teach students how to jive or dance the Charleston, for example.

Character cards

'I'm never going to remember all these people, Miss!'

When studying historical periods or episodes that involve long lists of figures, small character cards help students remember who's who.

Taking it further

The casting agency activity can be broadened out. Get students to create a pitch for a movie about the topic you are studying. What interpretation of events will the movie convey? Which events will be central to the plot, and what will the genre be? Younger students enjoy making movie posters for homework.

Whether it's the key players in the Wars of the Roses or the members of Mao's Politburo, students can really struggle to retain the names and details of the complex casts of historical actors.

Create an A6-sized card for each character involved in your topic, including a picture of the individual, key descriptive information and any particularly memorable or 'juicy' details about him or her. Try using them in the following ways:

- **Allocate one card to each individual** and make them the expert on that figure. Got a question about the Duke of Somerset? Ask Tia. Earl of Warwick? Ask Naz.
- **Give every student a set** to glue into their books or have a set on each desk, secured by a treasury tag for easy reference.
- **Play 'Guess Who?'** using the rules of the popular game in which players try to guess which figure their partner is thinking of by asking closed questions – in this case historical ones – removing cards as they eliminate people.
- Try the **casting agency activity** in which students decide which modern actors would play each of these characters in a movie of the period and have to explain their choices.
- Blow the cards up to A3 size and **display them** above the board.

Bonus idea ★

Get the students to create their own cards, setting aside time at the end of each lesson to make cards about the figures introduced, building up the set over the course of the unit.

Organising information and preparing to write

Part 5

Using cards to promote analytical thinking

'The card sort is a firm fixture of the modern history classroom.'

To help students to break down and make sense of lots of information, break it up and put it on cards. Vary what you ask students to do with the cards in order to promote deeper and different kinds of historical thinking.

Teaching tip

PowerPoint offers an easy way to make card sorts: make one slide for each card, then set your printer options to nine pages per side. Get the students to cut the pages into cards, and, having sorted them, to stick them into their books as a record of their learning.

Bonus idea ★

Your cards might, for example, detail the various events preceding the Sepoy Rebellion; describe the different features of life on a slave plantation or name the key battles on the Western Front 1914–18.

Grouping activities

Ask students to sort the cards into categories (for example, social, political and economic causes of a rebellion, or evidence in support of, or against, a specific statement). To make this activity more challenging, you might introduce subcategories once the initial sorting has taken place.

The most thought-provoking sorting activities involve students coming up with and justifying their own categories. This replicates the process by which we group information or evidence when planning essays.

Prioritising activities

Ask students to think about the significance of various information cards in relation to a specific hypothesis or question. After asking 'why did women get the vote?', you might ask students to arrange the cards in a pyramid or diamond shape, with what they deem the most important reason at the top.

Flexible thinking activities

Introduce instruction cards in addition to content cards to force students to deploy the information in a range of different ways over the course of a single activity. See Idea 11: Thoughtful historical discussion: speaking prompt cards.

Continuum lines

'Nuanced analysis is good analysis.'

Continuum lines are a fantastic way of sorting information or evidence in relation to a question, allowing students to see that things are rarely one way or another, but somewhere in between.

Suppose you are looking at the question 'Was there a Mid-Tudor Crisis?'. Students would simply draw a long line from left to right, with 'yes' at one end and 'no' at the other, and place pieces of information onto the line. Continuum lines are invaluable in the first stage of planning extended written pieces because students can identify patterns as they emerge.

While this task can be done on paper, it is preferable to put the pieces of information onto cards, allowing students to move them around as they work. If you don't have time to make cards, mini-whiteboards also allow students to change their minds.

Continuum lines and source material

Get students using the lines to sort source material. They should look first at the source's content, using this to place the source on the line from left to right to indicate how far it supports a particular interpretation. Having done this, they should decide on the strength of the evidence, moving it up and down, above and below the continuum line accordingly.

You can show students that the same piece of evidence can be used to argue different things. Draw two continuum lines for different but related questions, and ask students to use the same sources for both. This is particularly useful for illustrating how the strength of a piece of evidence depends entirely on the question we are using it to answer.

Teaching tip

There is an excellent example on http://www.classtools.net/blog/use-continuum-lines-to-arrange-a-scale-of-opinion/.

Once students are happy with their continuum lines, ask them to photograph them or stick them down. The result makes an excellent starting point for an extended writing task.

Ways with diagrams

'For me, turning it into a diagram just makes it click.' (Sabrina, 17)

Encouraging students to use diagrams or graphic organisers to present information not only promotes active thinking, it leaves students with notes that are clearer and more accessible than big blocks of text.

Teaching tip

See the online diagramming app www.gliffy.com for inspiration and to make a variety of digital flow charts.

The causation iceberg: When looking at the causes of an historical event, ask students to draw an iceberg with its tip poking out of the water. They should write the underlying or long term causes in the section of the iceberg beneath the water, and the immediate triggers above the surface.

Historical ripples: Katie Thoburn's idea involves drawing a stone dropped into water and surrounded by ripples. The stone is the event or factor being studied, and the ripples its effects – moving from immediate effects to long-term impacts.

On one hand ... but on the other hand: Students draw round both of their hands and write five points for and five against an historical statement by putting one point on each finger.

Flowcharts: Flowcharts are ideal for organising historical information, especially relating to cause and consequence.

Significance circles: This activity comes from the fantastic www.mrthorntonteach.wordpress.com. Give students a page of circles of varying sizes. Ask them to label each circle with the name of an historical event, development or person, choosing the size of the circle to reflect their judgement of its historical significance and making notes inside the circle to explain their decision.

Bonus idea ★

Get groups to create diagrams on a large scale by using masking tape or chalk on the floor, or dry-wipe markers or string on tables.

The 'e' word: making essays un-scary

'My year eights look terrified when I tell them they are going to write essays ...'

Use these ideas to help your students structure their essays, gradually building the confidence they need to tackle them independently.

To younger students, essays sound like very grown-up, scary things, and weaker writers often assume that they stand no hope of producing decent ones. Students need to be actively taught what an essay is, as well as how to plan and write one.

- Collaboratively plan essays by using the essay tree diagram (see Idea 59: The essay tree).
- Introduce students to frameworks which help them structure individual paragraphs. Whether you favour PEE or PIES (see Taking it further), it's worth emphasising that these formulae should just be seen as guidelines.
- Use a visual analogy such as the time-honoured burger in a bun (the top and bottom of the bun representing the introduction and conclusion, and the fillings representing the different paragraphs) to help your students grasp the idea of an essay.
- Take a long run-up to essays with younger groups by planning a series of lessons around an essay question and writing cumulative conclusions (see Idea 63: Cumulative conclusions) as you go. These can become the bases for paragraphs.

Teaching tip

It's worth emphasising that essays are simply the written version of the activities common to the history classroom which involve sorting and intelligently deploying information. Card sorts can be made to replicate the process of essay planning.

Taking it further

PEE:
Point: what is it you will say in this paragraph?
Evidence: the historical information that offers evidence to back up this point
Explanation: *how* exactly this information helps answer the question.

PIES:
Point: what is it you will say in this paragraph?
Information: evidence by way of precise historical detail
Explanation: an explanation of how that evidence backs up the point
Summary: a sentence referring back to the question showing how this paragraph has answered it.

Rotation squares

'In rotation squares, students examine the issue from different angles – quite literally.'

This activity, based on an idea tweeted by @mrthorntonteach, gets students working together to record their knowledge. It is an excellent revision task or can be used to help students plan essays collaboratively, as outlined here.

Teaching tip

Rotation squares are not only useful for essay planning, but also for revision, allowing students to make collaborative notes on four aspects of a topic.

Give groups of four a large A3 sheet divided into four quarters, with an additional box at the centre, as shown in the example here.

In their groups of four, students arrange themselves around a table so that one person is seated on each side, placing their A3 sheet at the centre.

Students write the essay title in the central box (leaving plenty of space underneath – this box will later accommodate their conclusion, too).

The four sections will contain notes for four paragraphs of the essay. You can either provide students with paragraph headings, or with time to consider what each of their four paragraphs will address. Though it messes with the formula, it's important to stress that they can include more than four paragraphs if they want to, by sub-dividing their sections.

Put a timer on the board, giving students about seven minutes to fill in the section of the rotation square immediately in front of them. They should use bullet points to note anything they think should be included in that paragraph.

Taking it further

Students will now need to think about how they can turn what is probably a fairly disorganised page of notes into an essay plan. See Idea 57: The 'e' word: making essays unscary and Idea 59: The essay tree for how to promote structured essay planning.

When the time is up, the group rotates the paper by 90 degrees, so that each person is now faced with a different section on which to make notes, building on the points already there. Once the square has been fully rotated and each student has contributed to each section, you can either move straight onto asking them to write a collaborative conclusion in the central box, or teams can visit each other's tables to seek inspiration from other groups and ensure they haven't missed anything.

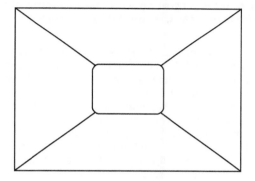

Bonus idea ★

'Mic drop statements' is a phrase used by Richard Kennett to describe those statements in historical writing which are so persuasive that they decisively end an argument in one's favour. Ask students to collaboratively come up with a mic drop statement for their central box. Every essay should include one. If this means nothing to you, google 'mic drop meme'.

The essay tree

'Don't forget those all-important leaves.'

The essay tree is a form of mind map or concept map, specifically designed for planning history essays. It couldn't be simpler.

Teaching tip

Students need large pieces of paper in order to plan in this way. I find that it works well as a paired activity, with sugar paper and chunky markers.

Students draw a tree as they plan their essay, writing the title in the trunk, the theme of each paragraph on the branches (one paragraph per branch), the evidence on the twigs, and the explanation of why that evidence is significant on a large leaf at the end of each twig. (You can in fact buy sticky notes that look like real leaves, and although this may sound frivolous it's often these little details that make ideas work so effectively.)

Not only does the essay tree help students to structure their planning, it's a memorable image to which they can later refer. Completed essay trees make good display features and can be referred to when first introducing younger students to historical essay writing.

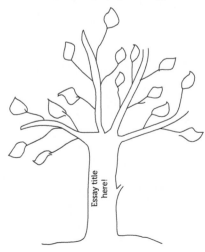

Essay title here!

Starters,
plenaries and
quick learning
checks

Part 6

In defence of (some) gimmicks

'Why is there a potato on my desk, Sir?'

Now and again, it's worth incorporating something particularly unusual into a lesson.

Teaching tip

Don't spend too long on these sorts of activities. Remember that they are mainly about energising students and piquing their interest.

Why did you love history when you were a child? For me, what is magical about the past is hit on by Hartley's description of it as 'a foreign country'. It is an alien landscape, a place we can try to create pictures of but can never visit and, because of this, it appeals to our imaginations.

Of course, using too many 'gimmicks' in lessons can dilute or hold up efforts to build students' knowledge and understanding of history. Having said this, I think we should make the most of young people's imaginations and innate curiosity, and sometimes the best way to do this is by 'grabbing' them with something unexpected or even fanciful.

Historical shopping bags

Bring some of the commodities you are discussing, for example, let students taste Spam, chicory coffee or other wartime foods when looking at rationing, and let them handle and smell real sugar cane and raw cotton bolls when looking at the slave trade.

Introduce a mystery

Ask 'what is this and what does it have to do with our learning?' about a mystery object. The objects don't need to be real artefacts. When looking at the public response to the Crimean

War, bring in some knitted socks or a balaclava; when discussing resistance to the Nazis hand out paperclips and when looking at medieval attitudes to disease, borrow the lunchtime supervisor's bell. Ask students, what could the connection be?

Create a crime scene

Make a mock-up crime scene to engage students the minute they walk into the room. This works particularly well with the police investigation lesson (Idea 27: Police investigations). You can use chalk to outline a figure on the floor when looking at a significant murder, such as that of Kirov or Thomas Becket, or put tape across the door to indicate that students are entering a crime scene. These things take seconds, but mean that younger students are immediately interested.

Get into character

Surprise students by starting a lesson in role. For example, play the Victorian schoolmaster when looking at the British Empire, or introduce the lesson in a different language when exploring the experience medieval peasants had in church. Again, no preparation or resources are necessary for this. I'm not suggesting dressing up...unless you want to!

Audio or video interviews

When studying something within living memory, why not make a recording of an older member of staff, or other member of the community, talking about their recollections of it? For years after I read them his evacuation story, even the most unlikely students enquired after the health of my Uncle Ron.

> **Bonus idea** ★
>
> Some of these activities can be offered to families touring the school on open days or evenings. Mystery objects and historical food stuffs work well here.

Quick progress checks

'Snappy progress checks help ensure that no one drifts off or gets left behind.'

Systematic checks on pupils' learning are an indispensable feature of outstanding history teaching. They allow us to identify and correct pupil misconceptions, provide directed support, recognise students' achievements and stretch their thinking. To gauge the progress students have made during a section of the lesson, or at the very end, try one of these quick progress checks.

Teaching tip

Those who need the most support may be the least likely to ask for it. As well as these whole-class progress checks, circulate and chat to more reticent students to make doubly sure that they are not being left behind.

Tell it in ten

Ask students to summarise learning, first into a paragraph of no more than one hundred words, and then into a sentence of no more than ten, forcing them to sift and prioritise. The ability to strip information down to the bones indicates that students have really got to grips with it.

Traffic light cards

A resource worth having in every classroom, traffic light cards consist of three small cards (red, amber and green) held together by a treasury tag. Get into the habit of giving a set to each student at the start of each lesson. You can then do an instant check on whether students are ready to move on by asking them to hold up the appropriate card, with green indicating that they've got it and red indicating that they are not yet comfortable with the material or ideas. You might ask someone holding a red or an amber card what specifically they would like made clearer, and then call on someone holding a green card to offer a response.

At the beginning/by the end...

Some topics have strong folk histories attached to them (think of the Gunpowder Plot or 'Bloody' Mary I) and this means that students approach them with differing degrees of knowledge and various preconceptions. Ask pairs to fold a piece of paper in half lengthways to create two columns, labelling the left hand column 'at the beginning'. As the starter activity, they should write down whatever they know or believe about the topic in this column. At the end of the lesson, get pairs to revisit their papers and label the second column, 'by the end'. Ask students to focus on the difference between the two columns. Not only does this demonstrate to them how much they have learnt, it encourages them to address their own misconceptions.

Taking it further

Once you have identified how much progress has been made, use this information to offer targeted support and extend learning. See Part 8: Inclusive history classrooms and Idea 12: Clever question stems for tips on how to do this.

Question dice

Students work in pairs, each with dice. The numbers 1–6 correspond to the words what; who; where; why; how and when. The two students take turns to roll the die and formulate a question beginning with the word corresponding to the number they have rolled. Their partner must answer the question correctly before taking his or her turn to throw the die.

What was the question?

If the answer is 'the Voting Rights Act', 'urbanisation' or 'Hamburger Hill', what was the question? Have students brainstorm in pairs. You can keep a note of the best questions and use them later down the line to check how much students have retained.

The exit pass

As they leave the room, each student hands you a sticky note or a short form indicating very briefly what they enjoyed about the lesson and anything that they would like more help getting to grips with. You might ask them to jot down their 'tell it in ten' sentence so that you can get a handle on what they got from the lesson.

Bonus idea

Kahoot

Kahoot is a free online tool that allows you to create multiple-choice quizzes. It's quick and easy to make a quiz, which you then display on the interactive whiteboard. Students log in to your quiz using a unique code and answer questions using smartphones or tablets. Go to https://getkahoot.com

The mysterious picture starter

'Powerful images grab students' attention like nothing else.'

Display a mysterious image connected to the learning about to take place, and ask students to generate questions about it, which they'll answer over the course of the lesson. The beauty of this activity is that students answer their own questions, and so clearly see their progress.

Teaching tip

Allow ten minutes at the end of the lesson to review the answers. If any questions remain unanswered, why is this? What kind of evidence might help an historian get closer to an answer?

Bonus idea ★

Assign different questions to different individuals or pairs who will then be responsible for producing and sharing their written responses. In this example, one pair feeds back on the question of where the bus was going, while another explains the impact the image had at the time. It is easy to differentiate this task by giving some thought to how you assign questions.

Choose an image that will get them interested, but one which leaves questions about what's happening and why. When teaching the Freedom Rides, I use an image of a bus on fire in 1961.

Give students five minutes to generate questions before feeding back and deciding, through whole-class discussion, which questions to focus on during the lesson. This is an opportunity to discuss the difference between open and closed questions, what constitutes an interesting historical question and why an historian of the Civil Rights Movement would, for example, be unlikely to ask what the man in the background had for breakfast.

Reacting to the photograph of the burning bus, students might ask: Where was it going? Why did it catch fire? These factual questions will be answered relatively quickly. Encourage students to ask more complex questions too, requiring them to place the source within its historical context. For example: What impact might this image have had at the time? Push students even further by encouraging them to question the process by which the image has found its way into their history lesson. This type of staggered questioning lends itself to differentiation. (For more ideas on questioning in history lessons, see Idea 12: Clever question stems.)

Cumulative conclusions

'This method means that we return our attention to the enquiry question at the end of each lesson.'

When you are working towards a specific assessment, or when your unit of study is built around an enquiry question, cumulative conclusions really help retain direction and focus. They are brief and digestible summaries of what has been learnt, framed in relation to a broader question and recorded by students at the end of the lesson.

The idea is that you end up with a bank of conclusions which, together, help students answer the bigger question. For this reason it's important to record them in the same place each lesson (the 'conclusion bank'). The back of the exercise book works fine.

If your enquiry question were 'Why did Henry break with Rome?' and you had just done a lesson on the spread of Protestant thought, your students would write a paragraph on how the latter may have played a part in Henry's decision, selecting only the key information from the lesson in order to do so.

Students will see how their learning develops in relation to the broader enquiry or assessment question, and can later use the conclusion bank as the scaffold or bones for an extended written piece.

Taking it further

We want students to be agile in their thinking and able to apply their knowledge in answer to unexpected questions (an important exam skill). If they finish their mini-conclusion ahead of time, you can ask the most able to frame what they have just learnt in answer to a slightly different question on the same topic.

Bonus idea ★

See also Idea 74: Ways of using index cards, where students record key information from each lesson on an index card and build up a bank of these to use in revision.

The exercise book glossary

'Choosing what should go in the glossary makes us look back over our work and pick out the bits we need to remember.'

The exercise book glossary is a page stuck into the back cover of students' work books, used to record definitions of key historical terms. It can be incorporated into a routine plenary to both check and consolidate learning.

Teaching tip

Avoid overwhelming students with lengthy lists of key terms. If you introduce more than two or three per lesson, they are unlikely to retain them.

You may have a predetermined list of terms students need in their glossaries, or you could involve students in the process of selecting them, setting aside time at the end of each lesson do this.

What to include:

Give some thought to the terms students tend to find most difficult, focusing on those seldom seen outside of historical discussion. Think also about the words or terms that students persistently struggle to spell.

Using the glossaries:

Encourage students to refer regularly to their glossaries. Try building the following activities into your teaching to help students become increasingly familiar with the terms:

- Incorporate the glossary terms into consolidation games such as pairs, tic-tac-toe or key term bingo
- Play 'what was the question?' in which students have only the answers (in this case the key terms) and must devise questions.
- Make mnemonics for key terms.

Bonus idea ★

Glossaries don't have to go at the back of students' exercise books; get students to make glossary bookmarks for use in their textbooks.

Glossaries are an important feature of differentiation in the history classroom, especially for EAL students, some of whom may benefit from translation of key terms. Discuss this with your EAL coordinator.

Plenary swap shop

'Give one, take one.'

This simple task asks students to distil their learning into five 'take-away' items — ideas or pieces of information — and to share and swap these with each other.

Ask students to make a table like the one below and give them five minutes to complete the top half. Then ask them to move around the room to complete the bottom half, with each new item coming from a different person.

My take-away items (things I have learnt today)
1.
2.
3.
4.
5.
Items from other people
1.
2.
3.
4.
5.

Teaching tip

Collect the sticky notes in and use them in the starter of the next lesson. How many can students remember without looking?

Taking it further

Ask the students to bring the five notes they have ended up with to a shared space somewhere in the classroom (this may be the whiteboard, a display board or just the classroom door), where they stick them. In order to avoid duplication, students must read the sticky notes placed there by others. What you end up with is a distillation of the lesson's learning in small digestible chunks.

What will STICK with you?

In this variation of the same task, students write their five points on five sticky notes. They move around the classroom showing and swapping these notes with other students until they have five completely different nuggets of information from five different people.

Board and card games for the history classroom

'The best way of revising.' (Luke, 14)

Certain games lend themselves particularly well to usage in the history classroom, not only as learning checks, but also as extended activities in their own right. To go a step further, have students make the cards and/or boards themselves.

Teaching tip

History lessons can touch deep nerves and address controversial or upsetting issues. As history teachers we have to make personal judgement calls on the appropriate way to deliver this kind of material; games are certainly not always appropriate.

Chance or challenge: This game is a cross between Ludo and Trivial Pursuit, and may be my all-time favourite lesson resource. Create two sets of cards: 'chance' cards and 'challenge' cards. Challenge cards carry questions about the subject, while chance cards carry a scenario and an instruction to move backward or forwards. In a game of chance or challenge on the subject of the New Deal, a chance card and a challenge card might look as follows:

Chance: You are a Tennessee farm owner, and thanks to the new dam your land will no longer be regularly flooded. Move forward 2.

Challenge: What was the role of the Works Progress Administration?

To make the boards, create a grid of around forty squares. On ten randomly selected squares write the word 'chance', and on another ten write the word 'challenge'. Players use dice and counters. When they land on a chance or challenge square, a fellow player reads them the appropriate card.

You can get the students to make their own cards, or provide them with chance cards without instructions and challenge cards without answers, asking them to complete the cards before using them to play. For a template, www.bloomsbury.com/100-ideas-secondary-history.

Snakes and ladders: Give students paper snakes and ladders boards (put the snakes and ladders on there for them, unless you want the lesson to turn into a graphic design session). Progress through the board represents the progress of an individual or a group in history towards a goal – for example towards independence or equality. At the bottom of each ladder students write down a factor which caused a positive change; at the top the ladder they write the result of that change. At the top of each snake they add a factor which hindered change, and at the bottom of the snake, the result. For a good, albeit non-historical, example, see www.tbalert. org/story/teaching-tb-in-a-game/.

Pairs: A simple game in which all cards start off face-down, and students take turns to flip two cards up at a time before returning them to their original face-down position. The object is to find a matching pair. You may ask students to match:

- Date cards to event cards
- Key terms cards to definition cards
- Statistic cards to explanation cards (I find this one invaluable in trying to get classes to remember dry statistical information to drop into exam answers).

Student-generated puzzles: Asking students to create crosswords is an ideal homework to help embed key terms (but do make sure that they have a list of the key words correctly spelt – otherwise the resultant crosswords can be rather too cryptic). Students can complete each other's in the following lesson. While this can easily be done with pen and paper, www.puzzlemaker.com provides easy to use templates to make crosswords, word searches and a number of other puzzles.

Bingo: Bingo is very similar to pairs in that it can be used to ensure that students can match key terms to definitions, events to dates and so on. To save you time on making bingo cards, have students make their own by choosing ten words from a list of thirty. Alternatively, try https://bingobaker.com/.

Bonus idea ★

Don't just move onto something else after finishing a game. Use the cards or boards as stimulus material for the next task. For example, can students write a description of the first Five Year Plan incorporating four of the statistics cards in their pairs sets? Or use the chance cards from Chance or Challenge in an analytic card sort activity? (See Idea 54: Using cards to promote analytical thinking, for more on card sorts.)

Super-quick games for the history classroom

'Throwing in a quick game re-energises a flagging group.'

Simple games help check and consolidate knowledge. The ones outlined here take little or no preparation.

Teaching tip

Avoid putting students on the spot when it comes to games, as some may feel exposed and embarrassed. Giving them 'lifelines', like bouncing the question to a friend, can help put them at ease.

Bonus idea ★

In Turbo taboo, include three progressively difficult rounds:

- **Round one:** Students simply describe the words, getting through as many as possible in a minute. Repeat round one until you have gone through the words in the hat. This is what makes rounds two and three possible!
- **Round two:** Students silently convey words to their teammates by drawing on the whiteboard.
- **Round three:** They may now use only a **single-word hint** to get teammates to identify each word.

Scrambled sentences: Students generate scrambled sentences summarising their new knowledge, muddling up the words before swapping with a partner and racing to unscramble each other's sentences.

Verbal tennis: Pairs bounce topic-related words backwards and forwards. Players concede a point when they pause for more than a couple of seconds.

Picture dice: Project six images or words onto the board, numbered one to six. Students in pairs take turns to roll the dice and tell their partner something about the picture or word correlating to the number they roll.

Tic-tac-toe: Create a grid of 3 by 3 squares on the board. On each, put the initial of a keyword. Divide the class into two teams. Teams win squares by guessing the keyword after a question or a clue from you. For extra challenge, get students to design their own grids and become question-masters.

Turbo taboo: Choose twenty words related to the learning. Write them on slips of paper. Put these inside a hat without showing them to students. Divide the class into two teams. Teams will take turns to send up representatives to pick words from the hat and help their team-mates guess as many as possible within the space of a minute, without ever saying the word on the slip.

Revising, assessing and feeding back

Part 7

Working with exam materials

'Mark schemes, examiner reports and past papers are your very best friends.'

Though the idea of working with exam questions, specifications, mark schemes and examiners' reports is not a new or particularly exciting one, I have included it because it is so vitally important for students facing public exams.

Involving parents

Do parents and carers know where to find exam materials? Create a leaflet to give out at parents' evening, pointing them in the right direction.

Bonus idea ★

Using examiners' reports:

- Scott Allsop suggests providing students with a bunch of examiners' reports and asking them to draw out themes or similar comments from different reports before collating these into lists of top tips.

- Richard Kennett suggests producing departmental examiner reports after mock exams. As well as having obvious value for students, this is useful CPD for teachers.

Using exam questions:

- At the beginning of a period of revision, get students to colour code a list of past questions with red, amber or green stickers to indicate how comfortable they would feel answering each. Use the results to shape your planning. Give students the opportunity to amend their colour coding as they grow in confidence.
- Using the same list of past exam questions, get students to group them by theme or topic, and then within these groups by type of question, to get a sense of the angles taken by exam boards. This is not the same as 'question spotting'!
- Use exam questions and example answers in revision activities (see Ideas 69 and 72).

Using specifications and mark schemes:

- Put the specification into pupil-friendly language and get students to stick it in the front of their books or files. Revisit it regularly to help students orientate themselves in the course.
- Similarly, interpret the mark scheme and put it into straight-forward language. Again, students need to keep this somewhere accessible. Use it regularly in peer and self-marking exercises (see Idea 71).
- Try 'preflection': students aware of the marking criteria record the negative feedback that an unsatisfactory answer might attract before even attempting the question.

Envelope exam questions and 'hot' essays

'One more minute!'

Jazz up longer writing tasks and recreate the urgency of exam conditions by breaking writing into short, time-bound chunks.

Envelope exam questions

In envelope exam questions, you give out a selection of long-answer exam questions written on envelopes (a selection of around four works well). Students open the envelope and on the paper inside write information. After two minutes, they pass the envelopes on. Once each envelope has visited four students (so once every student has seen all four questions), it is passed to a fifth student who is responsible for collating all the ideas on the paper into a structured written answer.

Teaching tip

You may need to assign more than one lesson to this, as the planning stage takes longer than you might think!

Hot essays (AKA pass the essay)

Collaboratively plan a full-mark essay in around six parts: an introduction, four paragraphs and a conclusion. You can get students planning in groups of six, or as a whole class using a technique such as the 'essay-tree' mind map (Idea 59: The essay tree).

Give each student a piece of A3 paper and ask them to divide it into six segments (by folding it or with a pen). Students will get seven minutes to write a section before passing the essay on when the time elapses (you'll need to put a timer on the board). Once the conclusions have been completed, revisit and discuss the mark-scheme before finally passing the essay to a seventh student, who marks it and assigns it a grade. This final stage may be done as a homework activity.

Taking it further

Get students to take a collaboratively-written essay home, edit and improve it and type it up.

The personal assessment bank

'Track progress at a glance.'

The assessment bank is a folder or booklet in which students keep all of their formally assessed pieces of written work, making it easy to track progress.

Taking it further

Use the coversheet as the starting point for discussions at parents' evenings. Once parents know that they can access a single page summary of key feedback, they can refer to it in order to support their children with assessments or essays set as homework.

I find this a particularly useful tool for sixth-formers, whose lever-arch files of notes quickly become messy and unwieldy, meaning that assessments such as essays are easily lost.

Ideally, the assessment or essay bank has a coversheet. It is helpful to create this in the form of a table, with the assessment titles in the left hand column, followed by a column for grades and one for feedback. At the beginning of a unit, complete the left hand column, filling in all the assessment or essay titles. This helps give students an idea of where the unit is going.

Each time you return an assessed piece of work to students, ask them to complete the next two columns by inserting the grade and a condensed version of your written feedback.

When you set the next assessment, give students their assessment banks. They should put the bullet point feedback from their last piece of work at the top of their new piece, before the title. This serves to remind them to act on it (it also helps you when marking, as you can easily see whether you have had to repeatedly give a student the same piece of advice).

The assessment bank helps to hold students accountable for their work because the cover sheet shows at a glance if there are any pieces of work missing.

Bonus idea ★

For younger students who complete their assessments in their exercise books, a cover sheet stuck into the book at the beginning of the unit achieves the same result.

Peer and self-marking techniques for the history classroom

'Student involvement in assessment turns it from being a process that young people endure into a fundamental part of their learning.'

The following techniques are tried and tested ways to build successful Assessment for Learning into history lessons.

Peer assessment

- **TAG: Tell** your partner something you like about his or her work. **Ask** a question. **Give** a suggestion.
- **ABC: A**dd something to your partner's answer; underline the **B**est bit. **C**hallenge your partner with a question.
- **Highlight the highlight:** Students simply swap books or papers and highlight their partner's best sentence.
- **E-editing:** When working on computers, teach students to use the review functions to comment on each other's work.
- **Spot someone who ...:** At the beginning of the lesson make a few students 'spotters', giving them the job of looking out for specific positive behaviours in their classmates over the course of the lesson. At the end, they feed back.

Self-assessment and reflection

- Give students ten minutes to respond to your comments on their work. **The PIN formula** may help students structure their responses: 'I am **pleased with** the following aspects of my work ...' 'I have made the following **improvements** ...' '**Next time** I will ...'
- Ask students to grade their own assessments before handing them in. You then mark it and comment on their comment. Incentivise accurate self-grading through praise.

Teaching tip

Many parents and carers will appreciate access to assessment criteria – make sure that they know where to find it.

Taking it further

For self-assessment and reflection, you could also use Idea 70, which asks students to write a summary of their previous assessment feedback at the top of their new piece of work, and 'preflection' from Idea 68.

Quick revision tasks for the history classroom

'Revision doesn't have to be boring!'

Many of the ideas in Part 6: Starters, plenaries and quick learning checks, also make ideal revision tasks. Here are a few more quick and easy ones.

Taking it further

For a treasury of easy-to-set-up but thought-provoking revision ideas, see John Mitchell's book in this series.

DES: Definition – explanation – significance

Students make a table with four columns (and however many rows you like). In the first column, they write key terms related to the topic being revised, using the following columns to define, explain it and consider the historical significance of each. This is based on a task from John Mitchell, whose blog www.jivespin.wordpress.com contains plenty more revision ideas.

Cover it!: Allocate a topic and a bunch of dry-wipe markers to a group of three or four students. They must cover a surface with notes on that topic in a set period of time. What makes it fun is varying the surface they have to cover – disposable table cloths or table tops (where easily wiped!) – work well.

Question and answer dominoes: This activity, inspired by an idea tweeted by Kate Jones (@87history), gets students off their feet and interacting when you need to reenergise them during periods of intensive revision. Students are each allocated a giant domino (just a piece of A4 paper) with an answer on the left hand side and a non-corresponding question on the right. Students must arrange themselves so that the correct questions line up with the correct answers.

Round the clock revision: This activity, from @Mrthorntonteach, helps students plan their revision over an hour. Put a small picture of a clock (with its twelve points marked) at the centre of a piece of paper and divide the page around it into twelve segments. Each section represents a block of five minutes: the amount of time students may spend revising each topic. See an example at https://mrthorntonteach. wordpress.com/2016/04/06/revision-o-clock/.

Exam question speed dating: In this activity, students move around the classroom discussing different exam questions with different individuals as a way of livening up revision and encouraging peer support. I tend to do this in four rounds, addressing four past questions.

Start by providing each student with four file cards. They will use one per question to jot down their notes. Every seven minutes, project a different past exam question onto the board. Students must work with whoever they are standing with to jot down the criteria for an ideal answer to this *type* of question before brainstorming content. When seven minutes is up, ring a bell or blow a whistle. Students must move to the next person.

Teach it!

'The idea that students can effectively teach each other needs to be treated with caution.'

We are often told that in the hierarchy of learning activities, the opportunity for students to teach others comes at the very top. But tread carefully.

Teaching tip

Try jigsaw reading – a strategy requiring students to work in small groups, dividing a text between them and then explaining their section to the other members of the group. (See Idea 76: Supporting reading.)

While it may be extremely useful for the student preparing and delivering the material, I've rarely seen those on the receiving end of a student-led presentation get as much out of it as they would get from a teacher-led or independent task.

I would argue that, as teachers, we actually learn much more about the material at the preparation stage than through the act of teaching, and that we can therefore harness the educational value of this process without subjecting students to each other's often nervous or monotone presentations. Here's how:

- Crowd-source (well, class-source) a revision guide: https://kenradical.wordpress.com/2013/04/10/crowd-sourcing-a-revision-book/.
- Get students to write comprehension questions as they read a text, and then swap readings with a partner who answers those questions. This works well as a flipped homework task (with the initial reading and question formation taking place at home in advance of the lesson).
- Get students designing textbook pages which you can use with future groups.
- Get year elevens to visit year eight or nine groups as 'option consultants' sitting with small groups and running through the content of the GCSE course. Do something similar at taster days and open-evenings.

Bonus idea ★

Encourage your students to teach content to their family members as a revision task.

Ways of using index cards

'Break information into bitesize pieces.'

Index cards are also known as file, summary or concept cards. They are small pieces of card, usually lined, used for storing discrete chunks of information. Their size means that students have to think about how to condense their knowledge.

Here are some ways of building index cards into your teaching:

- At the end of a lesson, give students ten minutes to summarise their learning onto a single index card. This is a great plenary. You can take the cards in to check understanding before returning them the next lesson so that students can file them with their other cards on the topic.
- Ask students to record their knowledge and understanding on index cards as a regular homework task. This is a relatively quick and straightforward homework task with obvious benefits for the students in that they build up a library of cards they can later use for revision. It is also very easy to mark.
- Get students to write super-succinct plans for past (or likely) exam questions by limiting them to a single index card per question. They should use one side to record the question and then outline the paragraphs they would include on the reverse.
- For more ideas, see www.wikihow.com/ Review-Using-Flash-Cards.

Students should keep all their completed index cards in one place – either by buying an index box or punching holes in the cards and securing them with treasury tags or hinged rings. The bunch of cards becomes an excellent revision aid that is both portable and durable.

Teaching tip

When it comes to revision term, give your students sticky dots in green, amber and red to categorise their cards. The stickers denote things they are confident about (green), things they just need to brush up on (amber) and things they are struggling with (red). This helps them prioritise and plan their revision, and students enjoy upgrading cards to the green category!

Bonus idea ★

Encourage students to extract just three file cards from their card library each time they sit down to revise. This limits the amount they try to retain in a single sitting.

Inclusive history classrooms

Part 8

Planning for an inclusive history classroom

'Every student needs to know that he or she is a valued member of the class.'

For students who have difficulties accessing and communicating information and ideas, history can be an intimidating subject. However, with the right planning, we can make history accessible to all.

Teaching tip

Don't miss the middle. It is easy to focus on the students who need the most support and those requiring most challenge, while expecting those in the middle of the ability range to 'get on with it'. Over the course of the lesson, try to ensure that you speak to everyone at least once.

Good differentiation in history lessons ...

... is planned

- Differentiation needs to be properly embedded into your planning process, not something that is stuck on as an afterthought. Not only do you need to know which students need extra support, but also the nature of their needs.
- One of the main reasons that students struggle in history lessons is language: in essence, it is a very wordy subject. So plan in ways to support reading and writing in the history classroom – see Idea 76: Supporting reading and Idea 78: Supporting unconfident writers.
- Plan your questioning. Effective, targeted questioning is such a powerful tool in moving students on that it's worth thinking of questions of different levels in advance.

... is about offering accessible, not easy, learning activities

- The limits of a student's expressive capabilities are not necessarily consistent with his or her intellectual capacity. One-size-fits-all differentiation (having one 'easy' worksheet) may limit students' access to higher-order learning. Like all aspects of outstanding teaching, the key to outstanding differentiation is to focus on the learning outcome rather than the process. If the aim of the lesson is to explore the interrelated causes of a rebellion, think about how you can make this realistic for everyone. No one is going to get there through a word search (even if it does keep them quiet).

... doesn't have to be laborious

- Instead of producing five different sets of resources, wherever possible go for activities and resources which can be interpreted and used at different levels. To revisit the example of students looking at the causes of a rebellion, activities like logic sums (Idea 5); causal webs (Idea 3) and hexagon configuration (Idea 4) enable higher order thinking surrounding historical causation and can be made accessible to all.
- Room zoning – in which you group students and ask them to do discretely different versions of an activity – allows you to deploy your support in the most time-efficient way.
- Many of the best resources for differentiation can be produced once and used every lesson – frequent word walls and literacy mats, for example (see Idea 80: History literacy mats).
- Good questioning may require planning but doesn't require any resources!

... pays off!

- Proper differentiation makes students feel valued, prevents disillusionment brought on by 'undoable' work and means that everyone gets to leave with a sense of achievement. For these reasons, it is one of the single most important ways to improve student behaviour. This, in turn, is good for everyone's learning.

Taking it further

Where possible, work with support staff at the planning stage. SENCOs and EAL coordinators will be able to give advice on how to make a draft scheme of work more accessible. Learning support assistants are often willing to take a much more active role and appreciate being given access to schemes of work and resources in advance of lessons so that they can think about how they will help students get the most out of them.

Supporting reading

'For some students, a page of dense text looks like a mountain to be scaled.'

First, we need to teach unconfident readers not to panic in the face of written information, then teach them how to get what they need from it.

Teaching tip

Teach students that productive reading takes place in quiet conditions. You can set the tone by playing some calm music, but select it carefully, bearing in mind that lyrics will distract from reading.

Make text unthreatening

- Can you offer some students a truncated version of the text?
- It is a good idea to **make key words and ideas bold**, or highlight them.
- Add vocabulary boxes to readings, providing clear definitions of difficult or new terms.

Promote active reading

- Try jigsaw reading tasks, in which different members of a group read different parts of the text and then come together to share what they have learnt. This allows you to allocate sections of various length and complexity according to students' reading abilities.
- Encourage students to approach texts armed with highlighters. For example, highlighting information about social conditions in one colour and information about economic conditions in another.

Teach note-taking

We want to move unconfident readers away from the laborious 'comfort-blanket' approach to note-taking (in which they write down as much as possible) towards an approach that requires them to process and summarise information.

- Provide students with a photocopied text on which the headings and subheadings are blanked out. This idea, from John Mitchell (@jivespin) is an excellent way to differentiate note-taking. After reading the text, they should decide what to put in the blanks by summarising the content.

- Use subheadings to 'chunk' the text. Get students to write the subheadings first, leaving space between them. Before tackling the text they should discuss with a partner what they already know, if anything, about each of these points.
- Teach the 'without pens, with pens' method. Students read the text once *without* pens in hands, and then write down only the points they have retained (however few), fleshing out their notes on a second reading.
- Try 'Cornell notes' (see Idea 77: Cornell note-taking).

Bonus idea ★

Ask students to summarise pages of their textbook onto sticky notes. These notes can then remain in their textbooks, making it easy for them to locate information.

Cornell note-taking

'Banish scruffy and disorganised notes!'

This note-taking technique, developed at Cornell University, involves dividing a sheet of paper into four sections, each with different functions.

Teaching tip

You may ask students to complete sections A and B in class, and then C and D for homework. Or, if you are 'flipping' your teaching (see Idea 10: Making time to think: the flipped history classroom model) A and B can be completed at home and C and D as the starter of the following lesson.

It is very common for students to struggle with note-taking, at least to begin with, usually because they endeavour to write down everything that they read or hear, and panic or become demotivated when they find that this is not possible.

The Cornell note-taking method offers a fixed structure and is therefore particularly helpful for those lacking in confidence or learning to take notes for the first time.

First, students should draw lines to divide their paper up into four sections as shown in the following diagram:

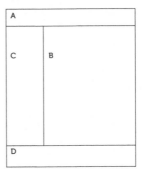

Section A: Identifying information. In this top section, students write the title of the presentation, clip, chapter, or whatever it is they are making notes on.

Section B: Free-form notes. This is the largest and most important section of the page in Cornell notes. Here, while reading, listening to or watching the educational material, students are free to record whatever information they feel is important in whatever way they like. It helps a lot if they can limit their notes to one side. See the bonus idea below for tips on how to encourage succinct notes.

The final two sections, C and D, are completed *after* the student has finished reading, listening to or watching the material and offer the opportunity to revisit and make sense of the free-form notes.

Section C: Key points only. Students should read through their free-form notes and condense them into bullet points, which they put into this section. It is essentially an extra-wide margin and the bullet points act like retrospectively inserted sub-headings on the main body of notes.

Section D: Summary. This is the final section, in which students think carefully about how to synthesize everything they have written so far into one or two brief sentences.

For illustrated instructions on how to take Cornell style notes see www.wikihow.com/Take-Cornell-Notes. For a simple student-friendly video clip see www.youtube.com/watch?v=ErSjc1PEGKE.

> **Bonus idea** ★
>
> Students will need to be taught to keep notes brief. Teach them common ways to abbreviate words and phrases and to omit anything they already know. For more on note-taking skills, see Idea 79: Sketch-noting and visual mapping.

Supporting unconfident writers

'The least literate student should be as proud of his or her exercise book as the highest achiever.'

Structure and guidance prevent the blank page being an intimidating thing. These are just a few ways to enable writing, from the most to the least interventionist.

Teaching tip

Frequent word walls and literacy mats will also support students in their writing. See Idea 80: History literacy mats.

Cloze exercises, otherwise known as 'gap-fills', are the most basic form of differentiated writing activity, and are useful for students who need lots of support, including those with little English. You provide students with a text which they must complete by inserting words or phrases into gaps.

Those requiring **most** support will need you to provide them with the words to go into the gaps. A 'missing word box' somewhere on the worksheet can work well.

To add challenge, give students the incomplete text five minutes before projecting the choice of missing words onto the board and ask them to work with a partner to guess at the missing words. You may also provide a word box with more words than there are spaces.

Sentence and paragraph starters will help those who lack the confidence to get going. They may simply point students in the right direction ('The Sepoy Rebellion resulted from …') or may give more specific guidance ('One economic cause of the Sepoy Rebellion was …').

Paragraph boxes help students structure their work, while giving them independence when it comes to phrasing. Each box contains a brief instruction and space for the student's writing, with size of the box indicating how much you are expecting them to write.

Bonus idea ★

Word-processors are the ideal accessories for those requiring most support, allowing students to manipulate text provided by you.

Sketch-noting and visual mapping

'To make spontaneous marks to help oneself think.'

In her well-known TED talk on the subject, Sunni Brown offers this definition of the verb 'to doodle'. Many students find that doodling, sketch noting and visual mapping help them to take in, organise and retain historical information.

Sketch noting involves transposing information to pictures, symbols, visual mnemonics and as few words as possible! The process of deciding how to structure sketch notes is an active one – students have to select, prioritise, organise and identify patterns in the content – and for this reason many find it more engaging and mentally stimulating than linear note-taking.

Taking it further

Other creative ways to represent historical understanding include storyboarding, cartooning, infographics and diagrams. See Idea 87; Idea 38; Idea 91 and Idea 56.

Bonus idea ★

Sketch noting and visual mapping are fantastic tools for the history classroom. Try the following:

- **Get students making group sketch-notes as a plenary, representing the lesson's learning**
- **Teach students these techniques as powerful revision and essay planning tools**
- **Give students choices about how they present their understanding of a topic** – with sketch noting and visual mapping as options.

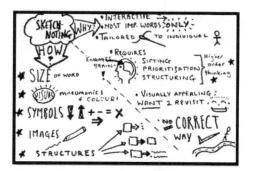

Visual mapping may refer to mind maps (in which branches emanate from a central topic word) or concept maps (usually used to show relationships between concepts and very varied in structure). Like sketch noting, visual mapping is an active process which supports learning by forcing students to distil and organise ideas and information.

History literacy mats

'How many different spellings of Goebbels do you come across in the average term?'

The easiest way to remind students of key spellings, basic grammatical rules and the principles of strong historical writing is by making history-specific literacy mats a routine desk feature.

Taking it further

Get students involved in creating the literacy mats: ask them to suggest which spellings or aspects of historical writing they find most difficult.

Literacy mats are a very simple tool. Simply create A4 or A3 laminated sheets which can stay on students' desks throughout the lesson. Students refer to the mats for spellings, useful phrases and even reminders about historical processes. It helps if they are laid out clearly, in a non-linear format, such as in a series of textboxes. An excellent example of a history literacy mat can be viewed at https://jivespin.files.wordpress.com/2014/01/how-to-in-history.pdf.

The following are just suggestions on what to include. In reality, every teacher's literacy mats are different as they are shaped by the needs of his or her students.

- Tips on sentence and paragraph construction
- 'Getting going' phrases or sentences – ways for reluctant writers to start paragraphs or whole pieces
- Linking phrases
- Comparison phrases
- Persuasive phrases
- Key historical words
- Topic specific words and names (not necessary if your students are making exercise book glossaries – see Idea 64: The exercise book glossary)
- Reminders on question technique.

More *challenging*, not just more!

'Extension tasks shouldn't just be about keeping kids busy.'

Challenge your keenest and most able students with questions that require them to look at the material from different angles.

There are some quick ways to build extension tasks in to every lesson which, once established, require absolutely no extra planning:

- Display big questions about the nature and purpose of history (see Idea 49) and ask students to consider these.
- Ask students to look for links with other topics studied or items in the news.
- Challenge them to include new historical terms in their writing (they can take these from their glossaries and room displays).
- Ask the most able to write less, not more, by imposing word limits to force self-editing. This actually slows them down by making them think about what they are writing.
- Incorporate speaking prompt cards (Idea 11).

Extension cards

Extension cards are an easy way to promote thoughtful discussion and writing. Laminate sets and hand them to students requiring more challenge. You can use the same of six cards for every lesson – students simply replace the 'X' with the topic being studied.

- Describe X as though to a much younger student.
- What was the immediate and the long-term impact of X?
- Explain how X came about.
- What does X tell us about the period?
- How important do you think it is that we study X, and why?
- How did people at the time react to X?

Taking it further

Particularly keen history students will enjoy a history club. Invite guest speakers, conduct local research and visit the history department of a local university.

Bonus idea ★

Try using extension dice as an alternative to extension cards. Display the questions and ask students to roll the dice to determine which one they answer.

Making history books accessible

'Getting them to read can be like pulling teeth!'

These activities are ways to help students of all abilities feel more at home with history books.

Teaching tip

Ensure that all students know their way round a library. This may mean taking them to the library for a lesson involving tasks that require them to locate books.

Have book boxes or mini 'classroom libraries' for younger students

Keep a box of engaging history books in your classroom and encourage students to get into the habit of going to the box if they arrive or finish before others. Include a range of books to suit all ages and ability levels.

(Re)teach sixth-formers how to read

Giving sixth-formers reading lists is fairly pointless unless you teach them how to use academic or reference books. The key is to stress that we don't really *read* these kinds of books (i.e. start on the first page and plough through to the last), we *use* them. Teach students how to extract the gist of a book in half an hour by:

1. reading the preface, introduction and conclusion, summarising each on one file card
2. reading the chapter headings, and, if possible the first paragraph of each chapter
3. searching online for reviews of the book (these often include a succinct summary of the argument)
4. using the index to home in on the information they are after.

Use 'proper' book reviews to introduce students to interpretation.

This idea comes from a Neil Smith training event. Expose a class to a range of interpretations of a topic by asking students to summarise different reviews as homework and to feed back in the following lesson.

Bonus idea ★

Classroom book boxes work best when the content is changed regularly. School librarians are usually happy to help with this. The books do not have to relate to the topics you are teaching – introducing a variety of subject material can pique students' interest in a period or aspect of the past to which they might never have given much thought.

Embracing diverse histories

'Education has to be something more than the reinforcement of the beliefs, values and identity which each child brings to school.' (Swann, 1985)

More must be done to bring diverse and global stories to the fore in our classrooms. The following suggestions are simple, practical ways to ensure more ethnically inclusive history courses.

Put local history centre stage: A paper from the independent race equality thinktank Runnymede, *History Lessons: Teaching Diversity In and Through the History National Curriculum* (2015), pays particular attention to the place of local history in diverse history education, highlighting the value of pupil research projects which get young people investigating the stories behind the demographic make-up of their local area.

- **Take the long view:** Focusing on history between 1492 and 1914 can reinforce a Eurocentric outlook. Looking at earlier millennia and at recent history quickly puts to rout any view of European history as somehow more significant than the history of other continents.
- **Confront the problem:** Initiate discussion about how history is written and how curricula are formed, and why this has meant that, until recently, history education has been lacking in diverse content.
- **Chip away at the artificial division between national and world history:** Take the time to put British history topics into their international context. Encourage students to ask, 'what was going on in the rest of the world while this was happening?'.

> **Teaching tip**
>
> Look at the history you already teach and ask how you can adapt it to make it more diverse, rather than simply tacking on extra bits.

> **Bonus idea**
>
> **Where to find resources and advice:**
>
> Runnymede offers ready-made lessons on many fascinating topics including Black Edwardians and the anti-fascist protest in the 1970s, as well as offering detailed advice on exploring diverse populations through local historical research. Visit www.runnymedetrust.org/.

ICT and outstanding history lessons

Part 9

Why and how? Using ICT to enable outstanding history teaching

'Are we going on computers, Miss?'

Too often, 'going on the computer' becomes the end in itself. Kids like it and it satisfies the endless directives from on high to use more ICT. The point of this chapter is to look at how we can use ICT most effectively to engage students and enable historical learning.

Involving parents

Parents and carers are usually pleased when they realise that they can find out about the curriculum and engage with their child's learning online. Don't forget to share at parents' evening links to any department websites, blogs or social media pages. (See idea 86: Using interactive ICT to bridge the home–school divide for more on this.)

Broadly speaking, there are five ways in which we can usefully employ ICT in history education:

1. **We can use ICT to make historical information more accessible and engaging by presenting it, and getting students to present it, in different ways.** See Ideas 87, 88 and 91.
2. **We should use ICT to train students in modern historical techniques.** Teach students how to search for historical information online, and how to use the results of their online research in a way that is responsible and conforms to academic convention. See Idea 90: Teach critical web-based historical research.
3. **ICT is a fantastic tool for differentiation.** See Idea 89: Word-processing tricks for the history classroom.
4. **ICT can be used to bridge the gap between home and school,** enabling 'flipped learning', offering students more support with their homework and getting parents more engaged. Ideas 85 and 86.
5. **ICT is a powerful hook.** We can engage reluctant learners by using ICT. See Idea 93: Virtual galleries for more on this.

Using ICT to achieve a 'flipped' history classroom

'Putting presentations on YouTube sounds complicated. I wouldn't know where to start.'

If you are putting off trying out the flipped classroom model because you think you don't have the computing know-how, you'll be pleased to hear that it's absurdly easy. The purpose and benefits of the flipped classroom are discussed in Idea 10: Making time to think: the flipped history classroom model. This page is a simple guide on how to upload presentations to the internet so that your students can watch them at home.

1. **Make a slideshow with a voiceover**
   NB: you will need a microphone for your computer (these are easy to find and cheap to buy). It is easiest to use PowerPoint, but there are of course other tools (see 'Taking it further'). Plug your microphone into your computer and then, in PowerPoint, go to 'Slide Show', and then 'Record Slide Show'. Make sure that you have ticked the boxes to confirm that you want to record narrations as well as slide timings. When you've finished, turn it into a video by going to 'Save As' and selecting Windows Media Video.
2. **Upload it to the internet so that your students can access it.**
   You may be able to upload your videos onto a school intranet or webpage. If not, here's how to put them onto YouTube:
   If you have a Google Account (it takes seconds to set one up) it will automatically log you into YouTube. Open YouTube and click the 'Upload' button in the top right hand corner. Locate your video file, wait for it to upload, and Bob's your uncle. It will provide you with a link to your video, which you can share with your students.

Teaching tip

For model flipped learning resources, look at Simon Hinds's YouTube videos: www.youtube.com/user/MrHindsHistory.

Taking it further

Check out Prezi, a different presentation tool that provides a welcome break from PowerPoint. It includes many additional features and can also be converted to video.

Using interactive ICT to bridge the home–school divide

'The ability to support students remotely is transforming teaching.'

In addition to making your presentations available to students online (see Idea 85: Using ICT to achieve a 'flipped' history classroom), it is now very easy to use technology to establish two-way communication with students beyond the classroom.

Discussion forums: Virtually all schools now have intranets, which, in addition to allowing students to access materials, usually include the facility to create discussion forums. Discussion forums let students post questions which are then answered by other forum users (teachers or other students), and allow them to hold online discussions and debates. If your school intranet doesn't let you do this, look at the free forum-building tools online.

The history class blog or Twitter account: Many history departments already have Twitter accounts, used by teachers to keep parents and students abreast of developments and to share ideas with other history teams around the country. Some teachers also set up Twitter accounts for individual classes to summarise learning, record homework and to share achievements. Blogs – very easy to set up at www.wordpress.org – allow you to do something similar and to include longer posts.

The advantage of class Twitter accounts and blogs is that you can update them *with* the students *during* the lesson, and doing so can be part of the learning.

Teaching tip

Internet security is paramount. Teachers or departments should never 'follow' students on public social media sites and should always keep their personal accounts personal.

Taking it further

Deciding how to summarise a lesson into 140 characters is a challenging exercise! Sue Cowley suggests this job be allocated as an extension task or reward.

Bonus idea ★

Edmodo: Edmodo is designed for students to communicate with one another and with their teachers and to access or upload materials in a completely safe social learning network. While many school intranets are still a bit clunky, Edmodo's interface is intuitive and accessible on hand-held devices.

Creative technology

'Variety is the spice of learning.'

Get students displaying their knowledge in different forms through various creative apps and online tools. Not only do they enjoy it, the process of translating content into new forms involves the valuable processes of organising and prioritising it.

Comic strips or storyboards: Free tools such as www.storyboardthat.com/storyboard-creator offer a wide range of prefabricated historical backgrounds and characters for students to choose from, organised by period. It's also incredibly easy to use, as is the simpler but more stylish http://stripgenerator.com/.

News reports: When creating historical news articles or reports, students can use online tools to produce professional looking pieces with ease. Try http://newspaper.jaguarpaw.co.uk/ to get students making front pages or, to create a still from a rolling news programs breaking a story, http://breakyourownnews.com/.

Collaboratively curated Padlet walls: With the online resource Padlet you can create virtual walls onto which students may pin digital images, links, notes or media. Walls may be jointly created by a whole class. The shared nature of the wall means that students can see and respond to each other's posts.

Information and idea mapping tools: Various free tools allow students to create mind maps, flow charts and other visual information organisers online. Try https://app.wisemapping.com or www.lucidchart.com.

Digital timelines: Students can create timelines with descriptions and images of the events using www.readwritethink.org/files/resources/interactives/timeline_2/ or www.softschools.com/teacher_resources/timeline_maker/.

Teaching tip

Much less flexible but too good to pass over, a Bayeux Tapestry creator lets students make their own versions of the Norman story at www.bayeuxtapestry.org.uk/interactive/BayeuxCreate.htm.

Bonus idea ★

Get students making content-based quizzes and puzzles for each other at www.sporcle.com and www.puzzlemaker.com, adapting or making memes to reflect their learning at https://imgflip.com/memegenerator, and even turning short summaries into jingles at www.ditty.com.

Virtual historical tours

'Go on an international field trip in ten minutes.'

Bring historical journeys to life by using technology to create virtual tours. Google Tour Builder allows you to move between and zoom in on locations on Google Maps. Drop place-markers onto the map and add captions, photos and even videos to explain the significance of the location marked.

Teaching tip

When studying the history of a region for the first time, use Google Earth to 'fly' your students from your classroom to the location you are about to study, via any relevant locations, to help them orientate themselves. This is useful when looking at developments or events which took place in distant or unfamiliar parts of the world.

Bonus idea ★

Where appropriate, try a virtual tour as a presentation tool in place of a PowerPoint presentation: it is more dynamic and less likely to be focused on text.

- Epic historical journeys such as the Long March or Columbus's voyage of 1492 can be recreated in virtual form. This helps students grasp the sheer distances involved and, because you can zoom in, lets you draw attention to the topography and ask students to consider its impact on events. I use a virtual tour to recreate the journey a letter from the New World might have taken to reach the monarch in Madrid in the sixteenth century to illustrate the problems created by the size of the Spanish empire.
- Use the application to understand the relative locations of a series of linked events such as the key battles of a particular war.
- Get students building their own tours. They can create 'virtual travelogues', putting themselves in the shoes of people in the past and detailing a journey taken by a group or individual. What would the virtual travelogue of someone on a wagon train headed west or a convict ship headed for Australia look like?

Word-processing tricks for the history classroom

'It can search, annotate, organise, classify, draft, reorganise, redraft and save that fundamental of the historian, the printed word.' (Ben Walsh)

As this quote from Ben Walsh indicates, the word processor is a fundamental tool of the modern historian and is therefore indispensable in the modern history classroom. But as well as teaching our students how to use them in their historical writing, we can employ word processors as differentiation and reviewing tools.

Enhance historical learning by using word processors for:

Sorting activities: Card sort activities can involve lots of teacher preparation time. Get students sorting virtual cards instead, dragging and dropping textboxes.

Assessment: Use the referencing and reviewing toolbars in Word to provide feedback on students' work, and teach them how to do this for the purposes of peer-assessment.

Source handling: Again, the reviewing toolbar is invaluable here. Get students to evaluate and cross-reference source material, inserting comments and highlighting sections.

Differentiation: Give students textboxes to indicate how much they should write and where. Have them delete, correct or move bits of text around. Teach students that the find function (Ctrl + F) helps locate a specific word or phrase in a seemingly impenetrable block of text.

Teaching tip

In *The History Teacher's Handbook* (2010), Neil Smith suggests pairing students for computer-based tasks, and giving them roles as 'pilot' and 'navigator', with the former operating the computer, with direction from the latter.

Bonus idea

Editing activities: The ability to manipulate and move text is what makes word processors such useful editing tools. Ask students to improve a dummy text, maybe one that lacks detail, explanation or balance.

Teach critical web-based historical research

'Some just print out and hand in whole Wikipedia entries!'

Inevitably, our students rely increasingly on the internet to find out about history. For this reason, we must teach them how to use web-based sources critically and responsibly.

Teaching tip

Encourage students to run their own work through plagiarism checking software: a number of free packages can be found online.

Bonus idea ★

Teach students how to cite web-based sources in history essays: See www.citethisforme.com for help.

Taking it further

Home in on Wikipedia. The many controversies surrounding this most popular of online sources make excellent discussion material for older students. For example, what are the implications of the fact that only a fraction of Wikipedians are women? See www.wikipediocracy.com

Provide web-based reading lists to prevent students getting lost in the enormity of the web and makes it easier for you to spot plagiarism.

Discuss the academic conventions around published history and the functions they serve: Show students a properly referenced piece of historical writing and ask them to find a webpage in which a similar historical topic is written *without* respect for these conventions. Discuss the potential problems that may arise.

Discuss the questions to ask before taking a web-based source at face value: Including who is or are the author(s), and how is the site paid for?

Ask them to locate several conflicting statistics for the same thing: Ask students to think about why we often get numerous and conflicting results when searching for statistics, and how they would decide which to use.

Get students to improve an irresponsibly researched piece of work: Give students print outs of a series of webpages. Create an example piece of work based on the information gleaned from these webpages, irresponsibly written in that it is unreferenced and repeats verbatim parts of the online text. Ask students to edit the example to turn it into a responsibly written piece of work.

Infographics, graphs and charts

'Data visualisation makes simple statistical analysis accessible to all.'

Get students using charts and graphs to analyse data, and infographics to make statistical information visually engaging.

Creative infographics

Representing statistics as pictures helps bring them to life, and numerous online applications are now available to help you create infographics: try Piktochart. Infographics often involve numbers being represented as images, the size of which, relative to other images on the page, helps the viewer easily interpret the information. Because students can choose the images they use in their infographics, compiling them is arguably a more active and creative process than producing graphs, and the infographics themselves are more subjective interpretations.

You can make infographics about any topic for which there is plenty of statistical information available. What might an infographic on the desegregation of American schools by state or of World War I casualties by combatant nation look like?

Charts and graph

Use programs like Excel to produce pie charts and graphs conveying information such as voting trends, economic performance or migration patterns. Not only does this strengthen students' IT and numeracy skills, it helps demonstrate the importance of numerical information in historical analysis.

Teaching tip

Graphs, charts and creative infographics don't have to be made electronically; creating them on paper offers teaching opportunities. For example, in a hand-drawn bar chart on the demographic composition of the Nazi vote, students can fill each bar with a short written analysis of the voting group's motivations.

Taking it further

Because the historian's currency is words, we are often too quick to abandon our critical powers when confronted with numerical 'truths'. Teach students to ask how and why a statistic was initially compiled.

Ways with word clouds

'The key words pop right out at you.'

Word clouds are computer-generated graphics which allow you to get the flavour of a complex and lengthy text in a matter of seconds. They make great display materials.

Teaching tip

When you are going to be looking in detail at an extended text, turning it into a word cloud and showing this to students before you ask them to read in depth can make it more approachable.

Generated from the text *you* provide, word clouds (shapes made up of words) give greater prominence to words that appear more frequently in the source text, making it easy to extract the basic gist. Simply copy and paste your text into the space on, for example, www.wordclouds.com and watch your cloud take shape. Here are some ways to incorporate them into your teaching:

- Put the scheme of learning or exam specification into a word cloud. The resulting cloud signposts the key content.
- Insert famous speeches into word clouds. If you display the photographs of historical figures muddled up with word clouds of their speeches, can students match the speech to the speaker? Ask students to compare word clouds: what do the inauguration speeches of two presidents look like when presented this way?
- Ask students to predict which words will come to the fore in a word cloud made up of an encyclopaedia entry on a specific figure or event.
- Try *Phoetic,* a cheap app which enables you to upload a photo of an individual and a related text to create an image of that person made up of words. Students' biographies of historical figures make ideal texts.

Virtual galleries

'Students become curators and critics.'

Students curate their own exhibitions of historically significant images, before viewing and critiquing one another's exhibitions.

I find this activity helpful when introducing students to the visual art of a specific period and when using historical images to encourage students to connect with a topic. When we look at the culture of Weimar Germany, for example, students create exhibitions including works by George Grosz and Otto Dix. When looking at the impact of the Great Depression on America, students select photographs from the Library of Congress's digital archive to compile their exhibitions. Having chosen their images, they write captions explaining the historical significance of each of them.

The easiest way to compile an exhibition is digitally, and there are some fantastic tools available to help students do this. The best available are Padlet and Russell Tarr's 3D Gallery Generator:

- Padlet is a simple way to collect images (and other digital information) online. It works like a virtual pin board, and may be edited by any number of contributors, making it the ideal tool for group or class collaboration on the virtual gallery task.
- Russell Tarr has created an easy-to-use, super-slick online tool (classtools.net/3D/) that allows students to create, and then stroll around, a life-like virtual gallery of ten images.

Teaching tip

Decide, as a class, the criteria for an effective exhibition, and then ask students to review each other's exhibitions. I ask viewers to note down 2-4 questions for the curator about his or her choice of images.

Taking it further

Turn virtual exhibitions into physical ones by printing the images and displaying the best in the classroom, or around the school. Cheap, second-hand frames are easy to come by and make the display much more

Visualisers

'Overhead projectors for the 21st century.'

Visualisers are little cameras that link to your computer or whiteboard. You can project a large image (moving or still) of whatever you choose to put in front of one. Once you start using a visualiser, you'll find that there are endless uses for one in the history classroom.

Teaching tip

The split screen function enables AfL by allowing you to compare two pieces of work, and combining the freeze frame and split screen functions means that you can show a piece of work before and after it is amended on the same screen.

Show historical evidence: Show an historical artefact, however small, to the whole class at once. The zoom function allows you to analyse the detail on objects such as coins, and the ability to freeze the picture means that you can pass an object around the class while continuing to display it on the big screen. Many historical documents – think maps or newspapers – are just the wrong shape and size to be scanned or photocopied. The tiny print often seen in historical documents is made much more accessible thanks to the zoom feature.

Demonstrate processes: Ever tried to show students how to complete a task by holding up a piece of paper and demonstrating whatever it is you want them to do? If so, you'll know that it doesn't really work. With a visualiser, you project a close-up image of your demonstration. This works particularly well when annotating source material or completing tasks which require you to move information around, such as card sorts.

Taking it further

You can save the digital images captured by your visualiser. This means that you can upload an image (for example, of a source you annotated as a class) onto the intranet or incorporate it in future teaching material.

Show students' work: Probably the most obvious and most transformative use of visualiser technology is in peer assessment. You can project an example of completed work in order to subject it to collaborative scrutiny or simply to celebrate it.

Beyond
the history
classroom

Part 10

History at the centre of cross-curricular learning

'If you want to know about humanity, you have to ask about the whole universe.' (David Christian, founder of the Big History Project)

Relating it to other subjects and to the wider world shows students just how important history education is.

Teaching tip

For lots of free, high-quality teaching resources, go to https://blog.bighistoryproject.com

Big history: There is a growing movement towards the teaching of 'Big History' - a multidisciplinary approach to history that places human experience on a much bigger timescale than we usually employ, looking, among other things, at human beings' interactions with the earth. It is worth considering embarking upon the teaching of some big history in collaboration with other departments in your school — particularly geography and science.

Forging links: Use staff briefings, bulletins or display boards to keep colleagues up to date with what's going on in your department, and initiate discussions about what's happening in theirs so as to find areas for possible collaboration. There is potential for history to enrich the teaching of any other academic discipline. Here are just a few examples of the endless possibilities:

Taking it further

At its most developed, cross-curricular collaboration might involve working together to plan schemes of work. It doesn't have to be this complex though: merely making reference to one-another's subjects in the course of our teaching helps students see the connections.

- Find out what students are looking at in English, art, music or drama and provide the historical context.
- Enlist the help of the RE department when you are looking at topics including the Reformation or the spread of Islam.
- Work with your biology department to underline the significance of various developments in the history of medicine.
- Draw geography teachers' attention to the historical examples of human geography you already cover.

Go on a trip without leaving the school

'There is something about doing it in a different environment that makes learning stick.'

Get out of your classroom and use other spaces around the school to offer students varied experiences.

Sports halls; corridors; playgrounds: schools are full of big, open spaces waiting to be used. Here are a just few examples of what you can do beyond the four walls of your classroom.

Giant timelines

Give students chalks and ask them to make giant timelines of whatever period you are studying. This can be done competitively in teams, or you can make a whole class timeline with different groups being responsible for recording different aspects of the learning.

3-D battlefield maps

When you want to show students the way a war or a battle developed, take them outside and have different groups play different roles. Use chunky chalks, or whatever you have to hand to mark out the space (I've seen a badminton net make an excellent 38th parallel).

Standing spectrums

Students physically position themselves somewhere in a line to reflect their stance on a particular issue. Ask students standing at either end to explain why they have chosen that position, and see whether they can convince any of those occupying the middle ground to join them.

Teaching tip

Children who don't find it easy to shine in the classroom may become quite different characters outside of it. Be bold and give roles of responsibility in these activities to those least expecting them.

Bonus idea ★

To illustrate just how immense the history of humankind is, give students a toilet roll, with each piece representing a hundred years, and let them create a giant timeline. They will see that almost everything they've ever studied happened on the last ten sheets.

Local history walks

'Clues about local history are everywhere; we just need to be taught to look around us.'

Encourage pupils to look at the immediate area through the eyes of the historian.

Taking it further

When designing interviews, initiate discussion about the pitfalls of questioning and the reliability of oral testimony.

Take your class on a lesson-long walking tour of the immediate area, pointing out anything of historical significance from any period. This is an excellent activity for the first term of year seven.

If you can enlist the help of other adults, it works best to divide the class into small groups for the walking tour. If each group has an adult attached to it, students may approach and interview members of the public about their memories of the local area.

If you don't know much about the area in which you teach (perhaps you don't live there), designing the walk is an excellent way to connect with the area and community. All local libraries carry books on local history, and you can make contact with parents and carers through the school newsletter or website to ask for suggestions.

Can't get out?

Bonus idea ★

Ask students to interview parents and carers about local history, using class time to design the interviews. You could set up a mini archive of the transcripts and audio or film clips they produce.

If practical constraints make it difficult for you to take students out, ask students to research and design hypothetical historical walking tours as a homework project. This could be done with maps and photos, audio recordings or even Google Tour Builder (see Idea 88: Virtual historical tours).

Outstanding history trips

'It is up to us to open students' eyes to the opportunities for historical learning that lie beyond the school gates.'

Though trips are usually lots of fun and always worthwhile, their educational potential is seldom maximised. Here are a few ways of making sure that you get the most out of them and ideas for follow-up tasks.

It's important to let students know what exactly you are going to be doing before setting out on a trip and, more importantly, why. It's difficult to communicate complex ideas with big groups when out and about, so use the lessons immediately before the trip to share the aims with the students.

Tell students in advance of the trip what the follow-up task will be – i.e. what it is that they will be making or doing when they return to the classroom to show and record their learning. They can then use their time on the trip to think about how they will approach the task. The following are some fun follow-up tasks:

- Students design visitors' guides for the attraction or location, focusing on its historical significance.
- Students contribute to a photo wall – real or virtual – including captions for each picture, explaining what it shows and why they have chosen to include it. (Padlet makes an ideal platform for this. See Idea 87: Creative technology).
- Students make postcards with photos taken on the trip and write ups of key learning on the reverse. See www.readwritethink.org/files/resources/interactives/postcard/.

Teaching tip

Asking students to do some background research about the location or attraction to be visited can help ensure that they are aware of its significance and have useful contextual knowledge. This makes an ideal homework task in the days preceding the trip.

Bonus idea

Enlist the help of PGCE students: they often have time and energy to plan outstanding trips.

Outstanding history homework

'Homework needs to be purposeful and focused. With a bit of thought it can even be fun.'

Homework offers the opportunity to build students' knowledge and independent study skills, but we often overlook it in our planning. The following are a few ideas on making the most of homework.

Teaching tip

Think about how you will monitor and support students who are working on homework projects. It is a good idea to set up regular 'check-ins' to ensure that everyone is making progress.

Differentiated homework: Homework can easily be differentiated by offering students choice in the task they tackle or in the format in which they present their learning. Give students a hand-out with three versions of the homework task on it, and ask them to choose the one they think they will get the most from. What is surprising (but heartening) is that students usually rise to the challenge and take pride in choosing to tackle a more demanding task.

Flipped jigsaw reading: The principle of flipped learning is that core narrative content is studied at home, ahead of the related lesson. See Idea 10: Making time to think: the flipped history classroom model. Try putting students into pairs or *small* groups and asking individuals to tackle different readings, recording their learning in the form of their choice before sharing it with each other (fitting it together – hence the 'jigsaw' part). This is obviously easy to differentiate.

Independent homework projects: Extended projects benefit students in all sorts of ways. I have found the following homework projects particularly successful:

- **Time traveller's guidebooks:** If you were travelling back to Tudor England or to a newly industrialised city, what would you need to know? This project, inspired by Ian Mortimer's wonderful *The Time Traveller's Guide to Medieval England*, gets students investigating the cultural context of the period they are studying.

- **Profile booklets:** Over the course of a half term, students complete profiles of key historical figures.
- **Rolling timelines or concept maps:** After each lesson students add to large timelines or plot their learning onto a concept map which grows over the course of a unit.
- **Local history research projects:** See Idea 97: Local history walks and Idea 83: Embracing diverse histories for more on local history and its potential to help embed diversity into the curriculum.

Taking it further

Offer a range of optional stretch and challenge homework tasks for particularly keen students and make the list of these tasks available to parents.

Planning for outstanding history lessons

'A goal without a plan is just a wish.'

The following principles are fundamental in ensuring outstanding learning in the short, medium and long term.

Teaching tip

Plan not just for students' learning, but also for your own. Both your subject knowledge and teaching skills need to be kept fresh. The history teaching community on Twitter (see the conclusion for 'tweachers' to follow) is a goldmine of teaching ideas and interesting historical news, while the growing popularity of teach meets is a good way to meet and share ideas with history teachers in your area.

Making 'best practice' routine practice

Certain routine activities are invaluable in helping ensure your lessons are of consistently high quality without involving excessive work. For example, glossaries and writing mats can be used every lesson to promote literacy (see Idea 64 and Idea 80).

The dangers of over-planning

When it comes to lesson plans, think in terms of sketches, not blueprints. Sticking rigidly to a plan means missing the many learning opportunities that arise in the natural course of classroom interactions. Plans should be 'roomy' enough to accommodate whatever tweaks need to be made in order to maximise learning. Similarly, medium-term plans should not be too rigid – you need to be able to adapt your aims and methods as you become more aware of students' needs.

Seeing the wood for the trees

It is important that individual units fit together into cohesive courses at each key stage, with long-term progression in historical skills and concepts planned for alongside the building of knowledge. As well as helping students hone historical skills, cohesive history courses should help students develop chronological understanding, make links across periods and draw out historical themes.

Conclusion

The online history teaching community is friendly, helpful and buzzing with ideas. Much of the discussion happens on Twitter, so if you don't have an account, consider setting one up. Particularly helpful history 'tweachers' include @jivespin (John Mitchell); @87history @mrallsophistory @littlestobbsy (Carol Stobbs); @mrthorntonteach @bennewmark @worcesterjonny @aheadofhistory @russeltarr and @kenradical. Many of these people are also the creators of excellent blogs hosting ideas and resources. The best I have found are Russel Tarr's www.classtools.net/blog/; Richard Kennett's http://radicalhistory.co.uk/; Carol Stobbs's https://littlestobbsy.wordpress.com/; Stuart Godman's www.aheadofhistory.co.uk/; Scott Allsop's www.MrAllsopHistory.com; and www.historypod.net/; and John Mitchell's https://jivespin.wordpress.com/.

History lesson plans and resources

www.runnymedetrust.org

www.nationalarchives.gov.uk/pathways/blackhistory

www.portcities.org.uk

https://blog.bighistoryproject.com

www.youtube.com/user/MrHindsHistory

OCR exam board: *Migrants to Britain, c. 1250 to present*

www.historyboxes.com

www.noisyclassroom.com

Historical images

http://punch.photoshelter.com/gallery/

https://archive.cartoons.ac.uk/

www.loc.gov/teachers/classroommaterials/primarysourcesets/political-cartoons/

Timelines

www.readwritethink.org/files/resources/interactives/timeline_2/

www.softschools.com/teacher_resources/timeline_maker/

Music

www.radiooooo.com

www.ditty.com

Newspaper templates

http://newspaper.jaguarpaw.co.uk/

http://breakyourownnews.com/

www.fodey.com

Creative apps and online tools

www.storyboardthat.com/storyboard-creator

http://stripgenerator.com/

www.bayeuxtapestry.org.uk/interactive/BayeuxCreate.htm

www.padlet.com

www.gliffy.com

https://app.wisemapping.com

www.lucidchart.com

https://tourbuilder.withgoogle.com/

https://imgflip.com/memegenerator

Piktochart.com

www.wordclouds.com

www.phoetic.com

www.classtools.net

Balloon Stickies

Games templates

https://getkahoot.com

www.puzzlemaker.com

www.bingobaker.com

www.sporcle.com

www.jdsbrainwave.com/trading-card-template/top trumps card template

Revision

www.jivespin.wordpress.com

http://www.wikihow.com/Review-Using-Flash-Cards

Book reviews

www.history.ac.uk

www.historyextra.com

Social media

www.edmodo.com

www.wordpress.com

www.twitter.com site

History teacher bloggers

Scott Allsop www.MrAllsopHistory.com and www.historypod.net

Stuart Godman: www.aheadofhistory.co.uk

Richard Kennett's http://radicalhistory.co.uk

John Mitchell: www.jivespin.wordpress.com

Carol Stobbs: https://littlestobbsy.wordpress.com

Russel Tarr: www.classtools.net/blog

Greg Thornton: www.mrthorntonteach.wordpress.com

History 'tweachers'

@jivespin

@87history

@mrallsophistory

@littlestobbsy

@mrthorntonteach

@bennewmark

@worcesterjonny

@Headofhistory

@aheadofhistory

@russeltarr

@kenradical

References and further reading

Alexander, C., Weekes-Bernard, D., Chatterji, J. (2015), *History Lessons: Teaching Diversity In and Through the History National Curriculum.* London: Runnymede Trust.

Carr, E. H. (1961), *What is History?* London: Penguin.

Evans, R. J. (2012), *Altered Pasts: Counterfactuals in History.* London: Little, Brown.

Mortimer, I. (2009), *The Time Traveller's Guide to Medieval England.* London: Vintage Books.